A View From
THE BOOTH

GIL SANTOS AND GINO CAPPELLETTI—
25 YEARS OF BROADCASTING
THE NEW ENGLAND PATRIOTS

JIM BAKER AND CHUCK BURGESS

Published by Rounder Books

an imprint of
Rounder Records Corp.
One Rounder Way
Burlington, MA 01803

ISBN-13: 978-1-57940-158-0
ISBN-10: 1-57940-158-9

Baker, Jim and Burgess, Charles D.
A View from the Booth
Gil Santos and Gino Cappelletti—25 years of
Broadcasting the New England Patriots

1. Cappelletti, Gino and Santos, Gil (Radio Broadcasters).
2. New England Patriots (Football Team). I. Title.
First Edition

Designed by Jane Tenenbaum
Cover and color insert design by Rachael Sullivan
Cover photo by David Silverman

DEDICATION

*To my wife Barbara, my children,
and my grandchildren*
—Jim Baker

and

*To Catherine Victoria; my Muse, editor,
toughest critic, and greatest supporter*
—Chuck Burgess

IN MEMORY

Dolores Baker, January 19, 1912 – February 11, 2008

Rita Sullivan Burgess, June 5, 1922 – June 11, 2008

CONTENTS

ACKNOWLEDGMENTS

Thanks

- Gil and Gino—our sincere thanks and appreciation for your cooperation and for allowing us to share your stories with your fans and admirers
- The Cappelletti family: Sandy—Gina, Doug, Julia, and Olivia—Cara Mia, Tom, Georgia, Angela, Lea, and Emersen—Christina, Jim, Ella, Jack, Brock, and Ava
- The Santos family: Roberta, Mark, Kathy, John, Jacob, and Hannah
- The Burgess family: Catherine Victoria, Cathy Ann, and Greg—Chuckie, Heather, Dylan, Quinn, and Annie
- The Baker family: Barbara—Kathleen, Henry, Owen and Oliver—LeeAnn—Tom, Linda, Kayla, and Emily—Erin, Mark, Elena and Joey
- Special thanks to Robert Kraft, Chairman and CEO of the New England Patriots and to the many individuals of the New England Patriots organization, especially Stacey James, Vice-President of Media Relations and Fred Kirsch, Publisher of Patriots Football Weekly
- Bill Nowlin, Steve Netsky, Terry Kitchen, Dave Schlichting, and the rest of the great staff at Rounder Books
- Marc Cappello, WBCN New England Patriots Radio Producer
- Roger Homan, "Ace" Statistician for the WBCN Patriots broadcasts
- The WBCN "Patriots Rock Radio" crew: Dennis Knudsen, Chuck Morrison, Scott Horrigan, Bill Bracken, Joe Soucise, and Jim Louth
- WBCN pre and post game radio hosts and commentators: Gary Tanguay, Pete Brock, Scott Zolak, and Andy Gresh
- Howie Sylvester and all of the WBCN behind the scenes studio and production staff
- Mark Winship WBCN Sports Sales Manager and Chris Rucker WBCN Ppromotions Manager
- Leslie Hammond, National Football League Director of Media Services
- Mark Katic of WBZ radio
- Tom Doyle of WROR radio
- And to the many other media friends of Gil and Gino who spoke with

us and shared their thoughts and stories about them and the New England Patriots: Eddie Andelman, Len Berman, Steve Burton, Joe Castiglione, Bob Cousy, Fred Cusick, Jack Edwards, Joe Fitzgerald, Dave Goucher, Tom Heinsohn, Bob Lobel, Mike Lynch, Sean McDonough, Al Michaels, Jim Nantz, Don Orsillo, Jerry Trupiano, and Bob Wilson

- Harry Laye, ardent Patriots fan from Lexington, Massachusetts
- The late Wilho W. Waukonan of Norwood, Massachusetts, who could be found at every game at Schaefer Stadium in Section 222—Row 3—Seat 1

Photo Credits

Thanks are extended to the Santos and Cappelletti families, Marc Cappello, and John Cronin and Al Thibeault of the *Boston Herald*. Additional thanks go to Scott Horrigan for his efforts on behalf of the authors all season along the sidelines, Bill Nowlin of Rounder Records and Books, and special thanks to Michael Allen for his photographs for this project as well as for previously released Rounder Books publications: *Love That Dirty Water* and *Golf Links*.

INTRODUCTION

NEW ENGLAND FOOTBALL FANS have been devoted listeners to Gil Santos and Gino Cappelletti since they originally teamed up as the radio voices of the Patriots in 1972. It is common knowledge that they are the fans' first choice to bring them the action at home, at work, in their cars, and anywhere else they may be—even in the stadium. When viewing the games on television, it was a time-honored tradition, before the digital delay of today, to mute the TV and to tune in Gil and Gino on the radio for the soundtrack.

The experience and insight Santos and Cappelletti have acquired over the years as they observed the Patriots go from perennial "patsies" to three-time Super Bowl Champions, is just part of the story of the men behind the microphones. Who they are, where they came from, and how they prepare and deliver their radio broadcasts so well—week after week and year after year—are all subjects that will be explored.

Through the good times and the bad, the broadcast team of Gil Santos and Gino Cappelletti has made the calls and analyzed every play of the New England Patriots for a quarter of a century. Together they have witnessed the Patriots win 17 playoff games, three Super Bowl Championships, five American Conference Championships, and eight Division Championships in 11 playoff caliber seasons. Gil and Gino have also suffered along with the rest of us, calling seasons when the Patriots painfully lost two Super Bowls, lost an AFC Championship, and posted won-loss records as dismal as 3–12 and 2–14.

A behind the scenes and inside the booth look at Gil and Gino in action during the history making, record-shattering 2007 *perfect* 16–0 regular season and the 2008 playoff victories in Foxboro highlight the second half of this book. We were also inside the broadcast booth at Super Bowl XLII (42) in Glendale, Arizona with Gil and Gino as they called the most disappointing season-ending game ever played by the New England Patriots. After calling the Patriots games during the best of times—a perfect 2007 regular season and the first two playoff games of 2008—Gil and Gino had to call the game that unexpectedly and in-explicably became the worst of times for New England—as the undefeated and heavily favored Patriots lost the 2008 Super Bowl by three points to the New York Giants, and with it their quest for football immortality.

Through it all—the good years and the bad, the wins and the losses—Gil and Gino have always maintained the highest professional broadcast standards and delivered their broadcasts with conviction, dependability, accuracy, and skill. They are simply the best in the business and this is their story.

Part One

GIL, GINO, AND THE PATRIOTS

1
TURN DOWN THE TV, TURN UP THE RADIO

"Gil and Gino are a legendary broadcast team and they work so well together. They're a shining example of what a football broadcast tandem should be."—**JIM NANTZ**, CBS'S NFL, NCAA BASKETBALL, AND PGA TOUR ANNOUNCER

"Gino tells you what's going to happen, but he doesn't come on strong. That separates him from the analysts on television. He knows what's going to happen. He should be in the Football Hall of Fame for his accomplishments on the field. I respect Gino as a commentator as do all the New England fans. When he says a play is wide open down the middle, expect it to go there. Together, Gil and Gino are excellent. Santos is very accurate. You can count on him. I'd much rather listen to them than a network broadcast because they know the Patriots so much better."—**EDDIE ANDELMAN**, VETERAN BOSTON RADIO SPORTS SHOW HOST

IT WAS EARLY MONDAY EVENING FEBRUARY 3, 2002 in New Orleans, just minutes before pregame festivities for Super Bowl XXXVI (36) were set to begin inside the Louisiana Superdome between the St. Louis Rams and the New England Patriots.

Patriots fans Eddie Lee and his son Alex of Newton, Massachusetts made their way to their seats inside the mammoth dome along with 72,918 other fortunate football enthusiasts. Within hours they would witness an historic moment in sports—the moment when the world's perception of the Patriots began the transition from annual also-rans to perennial champions.

The collective psyche of New England sports fans had been severely battered for generations. The Red Sox were still coming up empty in their 84th year pursuing a World Series Championship. The once-powerful Boston Celtics basketball dynasty was no more; they'd last won a World Championship in 1986. And the Bruins were hapless—without a Stanley Cup for over 20 years.

Up to this point, the Patriots had not done much better. Since their inception in 1960, they had only reached the "ultimate game" in pro football three times. The Patriots first reached a championship game as the surprising 1963 Eastern Division Champions of the American Football League (with a mediocre record of just seven wins, six losses, and one tie). On January 5, 1964, thirty thousand fans saw them lose the 1963 AFL title game at Balboa Stadium in San Diego, 51–10 to the hometown Chargers. After an improbable Wild Card AFC playoff run in 1986, the Patriots reached the National Football League championship game, Super Bowl XX (20) only to be blown out by the Chicago Bears 46–10 in the most lopsided Super Bowl to that date. In Super Bowl XXXI (31), the Green Bay Packers and their future Hall of Fame quarterback Bret Favre broke the hearts of Patriots Nation once again, 35–21, in the closest title game yet for the Patriots. It was close, but—once again—no cigars for the Patriots and their fans.

Legions of New England loyalists gathered in the streets and watering holes of New Orleans before the big game, especially within the 80 or so square blocks of the city comprising the famous French Quarter. They had to endure the taunts and bravado of extremely confident St. Louis Rams fans with the practiced stoicism of stalwart fans who had suffered without a championship, in any sport, for decades.

But those who had traveled to New Orleans bore within them some sense of cautious optimism. After all, the Patriots had closed the regular season with an impressive, if not improbable, victory run earning them the AFC East title and a playoff berth with an 11–5 record. Most fans harbored some hope that the Patriots were finally on the verge of a new era, revitalized under the ownership of Robert Kraft, the coaching genius of Bill Belichick, and the newly revealed on-field heroics of young Tom Brady at quarterback.

The road to this Super Bowl was a rocky one. During the preseason, the Pats were picked to finish *last* in the AFC by most national observers, mainly because of the dismal 5–11 record of the previous season. In August 2001, during the Patriots preseason, tragedy struck the team when 45-year-old quarterbacks coach Dick Rehbein died suddenly of heart failure. And off the field, the Patriots radio broadcast team of Gil Santos and Gino Cappelletti was disrupted for a time when Gino was forced to miss the first half of the season as he recuperated from bypass heart surgery performed in the wake of the loss of Rehbein. It was a sobering time.

Former Patriots lineman Pete Brock joined Gil in the announcers booth during Gino's absence. Though of much less grave import, Gil had some concerns of his own. "I was having a problem picking out numbers—I went and had my eyes checked and I needed glasses for long range. That was an easy problem to fix. But I felt that I had to concentrate even more on what I was doing when Gino went in for heart surgery—because now I didn't have my right hand.

"Now, I had Pete Brock, and I like Pete. Pete's a great guy and we got along wonderfully. But I knew then that I had to say to myself, 'Wait a minute now, Gino's not here. I can't rely on Gino.' I've got to bring Pete in to try to develop chemistry on the air until Gino gets back. So the first thing I've got to do is concentrate on what I'm doing in calling the game and give him less to worry about.

"See, when I'm calling the play and Gino wants to jump in and say something—fine. Because he knows what he's supposed to say. When he sees something that is when he says it. That is the way we always have worked. I've told him from day one—when you see it, say it. Don't feel as if you have to say something after every play. I told Brock the same thing. But Peter had never done a game before. So then I'm thinking I'm going to have to be extra sharp calling what I'm calling, setting the formations. I had the new glasses and so on...and I did more to lessen the load on Peter until he could gradually ease his way into the games that Gino didn't do. Eight games—half of the regular season. I knew I had to do more, I had to be sharper because I didn't know how sharp Pete was going to be. I knew how sharp Gino was."

The Patriots started the regular season with back-to-back defeats, losing quarterback Drew Bledsoe to injury during the second game. A brutal blow from Mo Lewis of the Jets damaged blood vessels in his chest and promised to sideline him indefinitely. It was far from the start of a perfect season. Things turned around for the New England team as 24 year-old Tom Brady took over for the injured Bledsoe and proceeded to lead the team to an 11–5 regular season record, and into the playoffs, concluding the season with an inspiring six-game win streak.

Gino returned to the radio booth rejuvenated and as vigorous as he had been during his playing days. He arrived just in time to witness the most exciting Patriots run in their history. Gil Santos recalled the feeling of having Gino back, "It was just like slipping on an old shoe. We didn't miss a beat—it was just like he had been there for the first eight games."

In the last game ever played at the old Foxboro Stadium, the Pats secured an incredible overtime playoff victory against the Oakland Raiders in a blinding snowstorm to win the AFC Divisional Game. Just down the hill, the new home of the Patriots was nearing completion and the looming structure hinted at great new things to come for the previously beleaguered franchise.

The Pats followed up the "Snow Bowl" in Foxboro with a dramatic 24–17 victory over the highly favored Steelers just as time expired in a hostile Pittsburgh stadium for the AFC Championship and a trip to the Super Bowl. The game at the new Heinz Field featured a twist only imaginable in a Hollywood fairytale as Brady was injured in the game and it was the veteran Bledsoe's turn to come off the bench to save the day and lead the Pats to victory.

In both playoff contests, it was a clutch Adam Vinatieri field goal that secured the win. Could the hottest kicker in professional football finally provide the advantage the Pats needed? Would a healthy Tom Brady resume the heroics he'd displayed before getting injured? Was fate finally on the side of New England?

When Ed and Alex got to their seats, they found a gift bag of souvenirs. Every single seat in the Superdome had a bag of souvenirs placed upon it. The gifts included a vinyl-covered foam seat cushion adorned with the red, white, and blue "Super Bowl XXXVI" logo. Was this an omen? The Patriots team colors were red, white, and blue, and an emotional wave of patriotic pride had emerged all across the nation after the horrific and devastating attack on the United States by terrorists on September 11, 2001, a mere four months before this game.

This Super Bowl extravaganza had taken on the role of a national healing ceremony with dozens of celebrities on hand to pay tribute to the victims of the airplane hijackings and the attacks on the World Trade Center and the Pentagon, and the crash of United Airlines flight 93 in a remote field near Shanksville, Pennsylvania. The decision *not* to postpone, cancel, or relocate this game in the aftermath of the most devastating attack on American soil since Pearl Harbor on December 7, 1941 was seen by Americans as a defiant and proud response to the national crises. To many observers, the underdog Patriots and their improbable playoff run seemed to capture the mood of the country at the moment and the red, white, and blue clad team became the sentimental favorite of most of America (except of course the St. Louis fans!).

To the millions who watched, listened to, or attended the game, the pregame ceremonies took on special significance, with the Boston Pops Orchestra performing the National Anthem and former Beatle Paul McCartney performing "Freedom," his tribute song to the American people, as the names of the victims of September 11 were scrolled on the giant Superdome video screens. New York City Mayor Rudy Giuliani, who had become a symbol of America's determination to recover from the attacks, was in attendance and was boldly making his presence known all over the city of New Orleans before the game. Spontaneous applause greeted him wherever he went during the week. The applause was for America.

President George W. Bush presided over the coin-toss before the game, the first president ever to do so in person at a Super Bowl. The fans in attendance were caught up in the extraordinary experience of having this game, a symbol of America in its own right, go on as scheduled.

In addition to the seat cushion, the other promotional items given away in the Super Bowl swag bags included a neck lanyard and plastic ticket holder adorned with stars and stripes, to preserve and display each fan's coveted game ticket. Lastly there was a small commemorative transistor radio with a set of "ear bud" headphones in the package.

The tiny two-inch by six-inch radio was a fully functional AM-FM device, but because of the restrictions inherent in receiving radio signals in the massive steel-reinforced Superdome, four frequencies were specially broadcast within the dome for the radios.

One channel choice was the Fox Television Network audio feed that permitted fans to follow the game as described by play-by-play announcer Pat Summerall and his sidekick, outlandish commentator John Madden—just like millions and millions of television viewers worldwide. They also heard the thoughts and opinions of TV announcers James Brown, Terry Bradshaw, Howie Long, and Cris Collinsworth.

The next channel on the radio dial gave the fans the choice of listening to the nationwide radio coverage of the game on Westwood One/CBS Radio Sports with Howard David and Boomer Esiason, and the third available station provided the St. Louis fans in attendance with the Rams radio network flagship station.

The fourth and final frequency carried the WBCN radio network feed from Boston and the play-by-play calling of legendary announcers Gil Santos and Gino Cappelletti. Needless to say, Patriots fans were delighted. They would be able to do something that evening that they would have done had they been at home in front of their television sets—watch the game with Gil and Gino providing the soundtrack!

The game itself was a roller-coaster of emotions for the Patriots' fans. New England had a halftime lead of 14–3 and in the fourth quarter led St. Louis 17–3. Then the Rams' vaunted offense—"The Greatest Show on Turf"—came alive and drove down the field twice, scoring 14 unanswered points to tie the game before the Patriots offense got the ball for the final time with just seconds left to play.

Television commentator John Madden told Fox's national audience that, with the ball deep in the Patriots' end, Brady would be ultra-conservative, "take a knee," and play for overtime. He was wrong. The Patriots would not try for the tie. No way! Not with Patriots' quarterback Tom Brady in charge! Not with Bill Belichick at the coaching helm! Not with the clutch kicker Vinatieri on the sidelines!

Watching the exciting action at home was veteran Red Sox radio announcer Joe Castiglione. "At that moment in the game I couldn't help but go over to the radio and turn it on to hear how Gil and Gino were calling the action. Nobody in sports broadcasting paints a better word picture than Gil Santos. And Gino explains things so well in that comfortable, folksy way of his. I always listened to them in the bad old days when the Patriots were down and out. I just had to hear them at this big moment in New England sports when the Patriots might be on the verge of making history!"

Gil Santos began his call of the final action this way, "It's been a heart-breaking fourth quarter for the Patriots."

"Button up your chin strap—here we go," added Gino as the Patriots, tied at 17 and with just a minute and nine seconds left to play, had the ball deep in their own territory.

Calm and collected, Brady directed and passed the Pats downfield as Santos—as calm and collected as *he* could be under the circumstances—called the action:

"Brady throws over the middle to the 21-yard line. The clock running to 1:09 to play—a pulse pounding finish to this one here!
Over the middle it goes complete to J.R. Redman to the 30-

yard line—41 seconds left, trying to get the ball into Adam Vinatieri's field goal range.

"Brady stands in the pocket, dumps it off to the left complete to J.R. Redman—30, 35, to the 40 and a first down!

"Brady stands in the pocket, steps up, fires down the field. CAUGHT! Troy Brown at the 40! He's to the left at the 37-yard line, and goes out of bounds! Stopping the clock, at the Rams' 36, with 21 seconds to go!

"Brady looks, fires over the middle—Caught by Jermaine Wiggins, down to the 30-yard line of St. Louis! The Patriots have to come up and snap the ball down here—nine seconds left!

"Brady throws the ball to the ground with FIVE seconds left!"

With the clock stopped, Adam Vinatieri jogged onto the field and over the Patriots Radio Network this Gil Santos call was heard:

"Ken Walter will hold, Lonnie Paxton will snap from the far hash mark angled to the left for Adam Vinatieri—a 48-yard field goal attempt.

"Set to go, snap, ball down, kick up, kick is on the way…and …it…is…good, it's good, it's good, it's good, it's GOOD! The Patriots are *SUPER BOWL CHAMPIONS!!!!!!!*"

Gil paused to catch his breath and then simply said, "Well New England, you have the best football team in the world right now!"

As Gil made his emotional final call of the game over the airwaves, Gino, sitting beside him, was briefly silenced as he took in what had just occurred. "I thought to myself of how I felt and then I said to Gil and to the audience, 'I know it's a great moment in Patriots history, but my thoughts right now are with all those teammates that I shared the building of this franchise with and how they might feel at this moment knowing what this team has just achieved.' I left the moment of the call of the victory for Gil as my thoughts at that moment went back 40 years to think of the guys who were part of the original team and everything after that in the '60s.

"For some reason I got very reflective, I mean I felt the excitement and I was so proud. But I was also overwhelmed by the magnitude of the moment. I thought about all the guys I knew back then, the games we played, and how we often struggled. And now here it was; the Patriots had reached the ultimate goal in football. But I thought I would leave that particular moment on air to Gil and I was going to go back to another moment. I had to wait to say what I felt out loud.

"We went down into the locker room after the game, which we don't do often. But after that game we went down and congratulated everyone. Every coach and every player we were able to meet, so that was part of the tremendous excitement we experienced."

Patriots fans went delirious with excitement and joy—St. Louis fans went numb with disbelief. The entire New Orleans Superdome crowd of 72,920 and John Madden were shocked—one way or the other. But Gil Santos and Gino Cappelletti were not. "We were not shocked, we were thrilled but not shocked. The way they had handled the snow game with Oakland, and then going into Pittsburgh and winning there, we knew you couldn't ever have counted them out of any game, especially this one," Gino recalled.

Listening to the Patriots on the radio had become a habit for fans, not only because of the quality and reliability of the broadcasters but also because for many years before the Kraft, Belichick, and WBCN era—it was the *only* way they could follow the team due to the National Football League's television blackout rule.

Brian McCarthy, Director of Corporate Communications for the NFL, explained the blackout rule. "It dates to a 1973 Act of Congress that allowed television blackouts within a 75-mile radius of the stadium if the game is not sold out 72 hours prior to kickoff. Until then, *all* home games of NFL teams were blacked out regardless of whether they were sold out or not."

An exception to the rule is when games blacked out in the primary market (Boston) could still be seen via a station in secondary markets (Providence or Manchester) even though they may be within 75 miles of the stadium. So it was possible to see some home games not sold out back then if you had a strong enough TV antenna to pick up one of the secondary markets. But for most Patriots fans the radio broadcast was the only way to follow the team if you were out of the secondary TV market's airwaves or were not able to be in the stadium on game day.

The Pats had a good number of home games blacked out back in Gil's earlier years on the air and dating to Gino's playing days, when the only way you could see the Pats play at home was to go to the stadium.

Otherwise, there was no TV and Gil's radio call was the only broadcast in town.

In 1974, the first season of the modified blackout rule, the Pats had two games blacked out and five home games were televised locally during a season that the Pats finished with a 7–7 record (each team played a 14-game schedule back then). In 1978, the first year of the 16-game schedule, the Pats had just four games shown locally even though they finished with a strong 11–5 record. In 1979, a 9–7 season, the number of locally televised games was again only five. In 1985 and 1986 (when the Pats did well with back to back 11–5 seasons), the team had five games on local TV each season. The Patriots' last blackout was in 1993, when just five home games were televised during that 5–11 season—the first year of Bill Parcells as head coach and the last year of ownership under James Orthwein.

McCarthy also pointed out how much things have changed. "Out of 256 NFL games in the 2007 season, only ten were not televised in their home market. That's 96 percent coverage. In 2006, only seven had local blackouts." Of course, there have been no blackouts from Foxboro in the Kraft era because all home games have been sellouts well in advance.

Since the inception of the team in 1960, the task of broadcasting Patriots games to the New England radio audience has been assigned to just ten different full time announcers. The longest reigning have been Gil Santos and Gino Cappelletti.

The inaugural voice of the Patriots was Fred Cusick, who partnered with Bob Gallagher and later with Ned Martin for one season on WEEI radio (then at 590 AM on the dial) until 1966 when Gil Santos made his debut with the Patriots. Santos began his career alongside Bob Starr while future partner Gino Cappelletti was still in uniform as an All-Star wide receiver and place-kicker for the Pats.

Gil's first tenure up in the Patriots' broadcast booth lasted for 14 years on WBZ radio (1030 AM). Gino joined him for six of those years, from the 1972 season through 1978, to provide expert analysis. In 1979 Gino accepted a coaching position with the Patriots for a few years and former Pats center Jon Morris did the color with Gil. Morris was the Patriots' rookie of the year in 1964, from the College of the Holy Cross, and became an American Football League All-Star six times and a NFL Pro-Bowl selection in 1970 after the AFL-NFL merger that season.

In 1980, WHDH radio (then at 850 AM) got the broadcast contract for the Patriots and installed John Carlson behind the play-by-play mike for the next seven years, with Curt Gowdy doing a one-year stint in 1987. Jon Morris remained as the commentator for both announcers. Meanwhile Gil went on to other broadcasting pursuits for a while and Gino returned as the Patriots' radio color man alongside Dale Arnold for three years beginning in 1988.

Santos and Cappelletti were reunited in the Patriot's radio booth in 1991 on WBZ and remained as partners when WBCN (104.1 FM) got the radio contract in November of 1994 and began to broadcast the games in stereo during the 1995 season. The addition of FM stereo brought a whole new dimension to the experience of listening to football. The crowd noise, and sounds of the game on the field—from the barking of signals to the smash of helmets and pads—made possible by the stereophonic placement of the parabolic on-field microphones, seemed to put the listener *into* the action instead of just listening to it.

Since their reunion in 1991, Gil and Gino and have remained the voices of the Patriots. The 2008 season will mark a quarter of a century of broadcasting the Patriots together.

Individually, Gil will have called the Patriots games for 32 of the last 43 seasons, and Gino will have been in the Patriots radio booth for 28. As a team, Gil and Gino have done an estimated 114 preseason games, 506 regular season games, and 25 postseason Patriot games together. Individually, Gil has done a total of 712 Patriots games and Gino has done 587. There is little wonder why New England fans prefer to listen to Gil and Gino as opposed to generic network broadcasters flown in to do the game of the week or a regional broadcast of the New England game. But in fairness to some of the better national announcers, playing to New England fans is a tough gig for anyone operating from the networks no matter how competent they may be and regardless of what sport they may be calling. New England sports fans have been spoiled, since they have enjoyed the play calling of a host of greatly talented and extremely articulate local announcers for the Red Sox, Bruins, and Celtics over the years. Curt Gowdy, Ned Martin, Bob Wilson, Joe Castiglione, Jerry Trupiano, Don Orsillo, Jerry Remy, Tom Heinsohn, Ken Coleman, Sean McDonough, Fred Cusick, and of course Johnny Most, all come to mind. Without much doubt, and with all due respect to the talents of outside television and radio announcers, most New England fans would rather hear Gil and Gino call a Patriots game instead of Al Michaels, John Madden, Jim Nantz, Phil Simms, or their colleagues.

Unfortunately, the once common practice of listening to the radio while watching the television broadcast of a Patriots game has been made very difficult thanks to, of all people, pop singers Janet Jackson and Justin Timberlake!

Just two years after their first Super Bowl Championship, the Patriots were once again in the National Football League's championship game, this time against the Carolina Panthers in Super Bowl XXXVIII (38) held at Reliant Stadium in Houston, Texas on February 1, 2004. Just as in Super Bowl XXXVI (36) the Patriots were ahead 14–0 at the half and saw a comeback from their opponents tie the game with seconds to play. This time the score was 29 all. Once again Adam Vinatieri was called upon for the winning points; again it was a long field goal that was needed—41 yards. Once again Vinatieri was successful and the Patriots had their second Super Bowl victory in three years. Exciting as that game was, it was the halftime show that many viewers remember—a halftime show that changed the way many Patriots fans enjoyed their games.

CBS was the broadcast network for the game and had contracted with Music Television (MTV) to produce the halftime extravaganza. It was a long way from the tame "Up With People" halftime show of Super Bowl XX (20) in 1986, the Pats' first trip to the big game. This halftime had a raw and disconcerting edge to it. Perhaps trying to be hip and to draw a younger audience, pop and rap music stars were put on the bill with disastrous results. Live and unedited, rappers Sean "Diddy" Combs (later known as "P-Diddy") and "Nelly" cavorted around the midfield stage grabbing their crotches before an alert cameraman or producer had the presence of mind to cut away.

The worst offense came when Justin Timberlake partnered up with Janet Jackson as the featured act. As both performers were singing, they made very suggestive choreographed moves. At the end of a song called "Rock Your Body," Timberlake reached over Jackson's shoulder and grabbed at her chest, tearing off what later turned out to be a "tear away" bra, exposing her breast and bejeweled nipple to millions of viewers. A landslide of protests and complaints quickly followed and MTV was banned from any future NFL productions. But much worse for Patriots fans was the decree that, starting with the 2004–05 season, all National Football League Games broadcast on television would be broadcast with at least an *8-second delay*.

As a result, if fans want to enjoy Gil and Gino as their preferred announcers for a televised game—as they had done for years—they now have to put up with a most annoying out of sync presentation. Because of the TV broadcast delay, they now know how the play turns out *before* they see it! Santos, very much aware of the popular practice of watching the television images and hearing the radio broadcast at the same time had this to say, "Well it is kind of a pain, but I think if you have one of those new television recording devices or options on your cable you can fool around with it to match up the signals pretty easily—if you know what you're doing." Actually, it's the live radio transmission of Gil and Gino's broadcast that has to be delayed to be in synchronization with the television and unfortunately, there are no electronic devices readily available to do that.

2
GIL—GROWING UP AMERICAN

"Gil Santos is one of the most professional and well-organized an-nouncers. He's right there with Dick Stockton and Len Berman. He has that rich baritone voice which is so appealing and as mon ami, he's always fun to be with. I know Gino best as a friend, playing golf, and he's a wonderful human being."—**BOB COUSY**, NBA HALL OF FAME GUARD AND GIL'S FORMER CELTICS BROADCAST PARTNER

GIL SANTOS, known to millions of faithful radio listeners as "the Voice of the New England Patriots" for over three decades and his longtime part-ner, Patriots legendary star Gino Cappelletti have an enduring bond that goes well beyond the team and their roles as broadcasters. As sons of im-migrants, each grew up in the environments of hard-working families with a keen appreciation for the value of a dollar.

"My parents were from Portugal and Gino's from Italy," says Santos, "and when you're a first-generation American, you have a different up-bringing than families who've been here for generations. You have a

Baby boy Gil Santos with his favorite stuffed toy—a kitten. Gil has had a genuine fondness for fe-lines his whole life. Photo courtesy of Gil Santos

combination of the Old World values and work ethic plus tradi-tions that are blended into your childhood."

As Gil and Gino experienced their early years, multicultural-ism was a simple fact of life. Gil recalls some of his childhood. "You celebrate July 4 and the Feast of San Antonio. You speak a different language at home. My grandfather, my mother's father, lived with us and didn't speak much English. So when I wanted to speak with them,

Gil as a young man in New Bedford with his parents Herminia and Arthur. Photo courtesy of Gil Santos

it was in Portuguese—in the house and to a lot of the relatives who had come over to this country at the same time. We spoke Portuguese, but outside the house it was English or a combination of both. As a child, I was bilingual and had an old-country work ethic. Right away you've got to work hard."

The depth of that work ethic becomes clear when Santos begins tracing his family's development with several colorful stories. "My maternal grandfather, Joseph R. Torres, grew pineapples in the old country and two big sources of business were in Germany and England until the First World War ended that and he decided to emigrate to America. I never knew my grandparents on my father's side, as my father, Arthur, came over [later] by himself at age 17 in 1920."

Gil's father and his two brothers, Jose and David, eventually settled in New Bedford and opened a small grocery store. As the original store prospered, the brothers established individual stores or businesses of their own. Gil's parents established a small family farm in the rural town of North Fairhaven, Massachusetts. "The yard was a paradise of flowers, fruits, and vegetables. My grandfather Torres lived with us and planted every conceivable fruit and vegetable you could grow in New England—corn, potatoes, carrots, and tomatoes—everything. And I helped him. He was the only grandparent I knew. After he passed away, I'd help my mother's brother Uncle Weber, who had a plot of land a couple of streets over and did farming. I'd go over and help him a lot.

"My father's parents died in the old country. They never came to America, so I never knew them. My maternal grandmother died of influenza when my mother was only 11. My mother, Herminia, was an only daughter, but she had three brothers—Weber, Joseph, and John that all came to America. My father had four brothers—Jose and David who came to America, Victor who went to Brazil, Antonio who remained in Portugal and a sister Isabella.

"I only knew one of my father's brothers, Jose, because David died in

1934. I knew all of my uncles on my mother's side. Everybody that I knew in my family worked very had to make it in America.

"From a very young age, you had to help. It was fun working with my grandfather. He didn't speak very good English, so it was conversational Portuguese with him and a lot of his friends because they maintained a lot of Old World customs. Feast days—eating fish, Christmas Eve. The food was 99 percent Portuguese style and I learned to cook it by watching my father and mother cook. Digging potatoes was the worst job I ever had in my life. I've always been picky about being clean. When you pick potatoes, it's August-September—very hot, humid—and you're digging in the ground with your hands. And sweating, covered with dirt. I was 6–7 years old and it was fun working with my grandfather. But when he told me it was time to dig potatoes... Picking grapes was different. You'd get on the ladder [and it was more fun]."

Santos recalled the story of how his father made his journey to America and found employment as a coal miner and as a cook—like many immigrants of the era, the elder Santos was willing to do anything and everything to make his way in this land of promise and opportunity. "That was a great story. When my father first came to America, he worked in a restaurant, then moved up to become a cook. The boat made two stops coming over—first outside of Rome, the second in Lisbon, and then to America—Ellis Island. He became friends with some Italian guy who said, 'I can get as much work for you and your friends as you want.' My father asked, "Where, when and what do I do?' He said it was in Scranton, Pennsylvania in a coal mine.

"So they went to Scranton and worked a week in the coal mine. There were all [kinds of] ethnic groups, broken up so they could speak each other's language—Portuguese, Italians, Czechs, Polish. But in this one area, most were Portuguese and Italians. And at the end of the week, the Portuguese were paid 50 cents less than the Italians and they said how come? They appointed my father to see the straw boss and find out why. He asked and was told: 'The Italians get 50 cents more because I'm Italian—and you're fired!' Just like that!"

"My father took the money he earned, went to New York City, and got a job working in a restaurant. He was there a few years and went to Fall River, where he met with his brothers to sign some papers for a property (their first grocery store). They went out to eat where there was some dancing. My mother, Herminia Torres who loved to dance, was at this club. They spot each other and start talking. But she was engaged. Two weeks later, after my father came back from New York, she came out of this mill in New Bedford where she worked and he's standing there. He says to her, 'Come with me. We're going to New York to get married.' She said OK and off they went. They were married August 10, 1927. She left this guy, whoever he was, in the lurch, at the post. My father would tell me that story and laugh!" Gil's brother, Arthur Jr., was the first-born son of Arthur and Herminia. Young Gil came along 10 years after that. "I was born April 19, 1938—Patriots Day. So I'm the only person in America who can make this claim: Ready? I was born on Patriots Day, married on Patriots Day (April 19, 1961), and I'm the voice of the Patriots!"

Gil first met his wife Roberta (Reul) in the mid 1950s at a beach in Fairhaven, Massachusetts when she was just 14 years old. He was 16. About three weeks after their seaside encounter, Gil enlisted a buddy who had a car, and he tracked down Roberta at her New Bedford home hoping to continue their relationship. Gil pursued Roberta even though her parents thought she was too young to date. According to Roberta, "He was told to go home and to stop being such a nuisance!" The fledgling courtship was put on hold for several years until Gil entered Southeastern Massachusetts University in nearby North Dartmouth and Roberta was a senior at New Bedford High School. Gil, then 19, met Roberta again at a record hop, referred to locally as the "Y" Dance, held every Friday night at the New Bedford YMCA. They began to date. Unfortunately, at the time Roberta was also seeing one of Gil's fraternity brothers from SMU (now the University of Massachusetts at Dartmouth) and "that made for some sticky situations when it came time to asking me out for fraternity dances or for homecoming," Roberta recalled with a smile. Gil prevailed and they courted, for real this time, until he and Roberta got married in 1961.

A proud Gil Santos and his bride Roberta on their wedding day—Patriots Day 1961! Gil was born on Patriots Day, was married on Patriots Day, and became the voice of the Patriots for over 32 years. Photo courtesy of Gil Santos

Santos' broadcasting start was at radio station WBSM in New

Gil's first radio broadcasting job was calling high school basketball games in New
Bedford. Photo courtesy of Gil Santos

Gil on active duty at Fort Bragg, NC, during the Cold
War. Photo courtesy of Gil Santos

Bedford, Massachusetts where he worked part-time weekends and was
a summer replacement during his college years. "In 1958, I asked Hal
Peterson, the announcer on WBSM, if I could go with him to a high
school basketball game. I'd told him I wanted to learn by watching. Hal
said I could go along with him. I'll never forget, it was a Brockton-New
Bedford game." And that was the start of his on-the-job training for the
career he has had all his life.

Santos served a year in the Army with the First Howitzer Battalion—
211th Field Artillery in 1961. He recalled his military days; "I joined the
Mass Army National Guard on August 6, 1961. A few days later the Russians put up the Berlin Wall and a few days after that, my unit was acti-
vated. We went on active duty right away and while the paper work was
being done and the barracks were being readied at Ft. Bragg, North
Carolina, we reported to duty each day in New Bedford...that's when
we would march through the streets of the city to restaurants around the
area for our three meals each day...marching to and from the restaurants with the top sergeant barking out cadence and the troops singing
songs. Of course the result was that we were waking up everybody in the
area at 6 a.m. as we marched our way to a local place for breakfast each
day! In September we went to Ft. Bragg and stayed there as artillery
support for the 82nd Airborne Division until our release from active
duty in September of 1962."

Gil finished his active duty and finished his military obligation in the
reserves with the Army National Guard while he took up his radio job

full time at WBSM in 1962. Shortly after that, in 1963, son Mark was born and now Gil had a family, a job in broadcasting, and a continuing military obligation during the Cold War. "I stayed in the Guard reaching the rank of staff sergeant and was in charge of a 155 MM gun crew. I was discharged in 1967." Gil's discharge from the National Guard coincided with the birth of the second Santos baby, daughter Kathy.

Left: Gil calling the Pats in the WBZ radio booth with his first Patriots broadcasting partner Bob Starr. Photo courtesy of Gil Santos

Right: Gil and Gino first teamed up as the voices of both Boston College and The New England Patriots during the 1970s. Photo courtesy of Gino Cappelletti

GIL SANTOS & GINO CAPPELLETTI

BROADCASTERS FOR

BOSTON COLLEGE EAGLES
&
NEW ENGLAND PATRIOTS

WBZ RADIO 1030 ₩

In 1966 Santos went from local radio in and around his hometown area to the major market station of WBZ in Boston. Santos is still with the 50,000-watt radio station, a relationship of over 42 years! Gil is still doing about 2,500 sports reports and commentaries a year. He is the station's sports director and is on the air from 6 a.m. to at least 10 a.m., then tapes his segments for later sportscasts. He estimates that he has probably done "close to 100,000 sportscasts, reports, and commentaries" in his career.

Santos' broadcasting work has brought him to many stadiums, arenas, and other sports venues across the nation during his interesting and varied career. He called his first Patriots action from 1966–1979 on WBZ and returned to the Foxboro broadcast booth on WBCN-FM from 1991 to the present. Gil teamed up with his current partner Gino Cappelletti in 1972 and again in 1991 for over two decades of broadcasting Patriots football together.

Gil also called Boston College football for 15 years, the bulk from 1968–1977, and some in the late 1980s to early 1990s. Gino was his partner for seven of those Boston College broadcast seasons, from 1972–1978. Gil and Gino also teamed up in the spring and summer of 1983, calling the short-lived Boston Breakers' football games on WBZ radio. Santos even called some NIT tourney basketball with Chuck Chevalier.

He called Penn State football from 1983 through 1986 with John Grant and did a show with longtime Penn State head coach Joe Paterno and his brother George. The roundtable show aired Friday nights with

Gil and his family enjoy a moment at home during the busy 1970s when Gil was calling both the Patriots and Boston College football games on WBZ radio. Gil holds the ball for son Mark while daughter Kathy and Roberta look on. Photo courtesy of Gil Santos

Joe and also Steve Jones, Grant and Stan Savran. Santos recalls that once a year "Joe would have us to his home for spaghetti and football talk that would last for hours and hours." How Gil Santos, a Boston based broadcaster, got connected with calling the football games for the State University in Pennsylvania is an interesting story. How he actually got there to do the job is even better. "What happened was we had lost the broadcasting contract with Patriots here at WBZ and we had lost Boston College as well. In 1983 the Breakers came into existence as the Boston franchise for the new United States Football League (USFL), playing at Boston University's Nickerson Field. Gino and I did the games on WBZ for the one season they were in Boston. The Breakers played in the spring and summer so as not to go head-on with the NFL or college football. By then I was also doing the Celtics on television. But doing another season of football on the radio really whetted my appetite once again and made me realize while I really enjoyed doing the Celtics on television, doing football on the radio was what I loved more than anything else. I happened to read that the long-time voice at Penn State, Fran Fisher was retiring. The guy that was the General Manager at WBZ at the time had worked as the GM at WKDK and they carried Penn State football. So I got a contact name and was told to send in a tape. Within two or three days I was called and was told the job was mine if I wanted it.

"Of course, I said yes and I started my time with Penn State in the fall of 1983. What I would do is fly out of Boston on a Friday to Pittsburgh, from Pittsburgh take a puddle jumper over to State College, stay in State College Friday night, do the Penn State game Saturday afternoon, stay overnight in State College Saturday night, take a puddle jumper to Pittsburgh on Sunday morning, and come home Sunday afternoon or evening. When they played out of town, I just flew to wherever the game was. The longest game was in Honolulu. I had to leave on Christmas day. We played in the Hula Bowl against the University of Washington (December 26, 1983). We won the game 13–10.

"Now it got to be a problem when the Celtics season started because there were times when I would have a Celtics game at night and a Penn State game in the afternoon—in different places. So I ended up chartering small planes. I think I ran into that problem three different times. Penn State had played Cincinnati on Saturday afternoon; the Celts were playing the Pistons in Pontiac, Michigan on Saturday night. I chartered a plane from the Cincinnati airport, to Pontiac and had a car race me to

Gil teamed up once again with Gino during the spring and summer of 1983 calling the action of the Boston Breakers of the short-lived United States Football League. (Left to right) WBZ general manager Bill Hartman, Gil, Breakers president Bob Caporale, and Gino. Photo courtesy of Gino Cappelletti

the arena. Two other times it was out of Penn State. I chartered a plane from State College to get me to a Celtics game in Baltimore and I think Atlanta was the other."

Of all the broadcasting assignments Santos has had in his long career, calling the Boston Marathon on WBZ radio for the past 38 straight years has been the most challenging.

"The Marathon is the most difficult sportscasting assignment a radio guy could possibly try to do. Everything's taking place *miles away!*

"You are relying on a dozen reporters out in the field, a guy on a truck, a guy in a helicopter. Now lately they have been going on live television and that helps you see what's going on. But you're going from place to place to place—you're talking with two other people in the booth at the finish line and in my other ear, my producer is telling me where to go next, to one of many other reporter locations along the route. Your mind is going 500 miles per hour for two and a half hours trying to tie it all together—something that began 26 miles from where I am—and you don't really *see it* until the last 30 seconds!"

Gil's longstanding cohorts at WBZ included the recently retired newsman and broadcasting great Gary LaPierre. Gil worked alongside Gary for over 35 years "There wasn't one cross word ever between us," Gil says. Legendary personality Carl DeSuze became another colleague in 1971, when Gil started. DeSuze retired in the 1980s. Another Boston radio institution, Dave Maynard, was a morning teammate of Gil for over 20 years.

Santos' career brought him to the National Basketball Association for 10 seasons from 1980 to 1990 calling Boston Celtics games on Boston television stations Channel 4 and Channel 56—five years at each outlet. He also filled in for Johnny Most on radio for a stretch when Most had throat trouble in the 1970s. Santos would work the first half, Most the second half.

Celtics great Bob Cousy was Gil's partner on television; on other occasions, Gil partnered with the affable Satch Sanders behind the mike. As with the Santos-Cappelletti partnership today, his teaming with the "Cooz" was also a close friendship—so close that they regularly called each other "mon ami" on the air in conversations between calls. "We had a good rapport. Cooz's parents were born in France and Cooz was either born there or born on the way over to America. He would occasionally toss in something French and one day he said to me, 'Mon ami...' I thought it was funny so I started calling him mon ami. People would ask me, 'Hey, how's mon ami?' That started more than 25 years ago, but mon ami has stuck to this day.

"One night, Cooz was visiting his mother. She was elderly and I'm not sure if she was in a nursing home or hospital. But Cooz went to visit her and she said to him, 'I didn't know Gil Santos was French.' Cooz said, 'He's not.' And she said, 'Well, he calls you mon ami all the time—Mon ami, Robert!' She thought I was French."

Another story: "You know basketball life is crazy because you're doing so many trips. You're in and out, up at crazy hours, play a game here today and someplace else tomorrow. We went on the air one night with a standup live shot. The red light went on and I said, 'Good evening, everyone.' And I couldn't remember where I was. I just stopped for a moment, turned and said, 'Cooz, where are we?' He put his arm around me and said, 'We're in Atlanta, mon ami.' I didn't know where the hell I was. We'd played in Indiana, Washington, or someplace the night before.

"Those Celtics teams were great. The '86 team was one of the greatest of all-time—won 22 in a row, something like that. As I mentioned before, I had a Penn State football game in Cincinnati on a Saturday afternoon and a Celtics game in Pontiac, Michigan that night. So I had to charter a plane. Of course I had to do that several times, but this one I really remember because of the weather. Before the game, I hired a cab and told him to meet me at the press elevator outside Riverfront Stadium. The football game ends around three o'clock. I leave the post-game show to my color guys, run like hell downstairs, and jump in the cab.

"He races me to the airport, which is in Kentucky. I jump into this small Piper Cub-like plane. This is in November. This guy takes off, he's flying along and says there's a big storm ahead. He said he'd fly around it and I said, 'If you do that, I'd never make the game.' He said, 'Well, I'll try to get through some of it and if it gets too bad, I'll have to go around it.' So we go through snow and sleet coming down and you couldn't see more that an arms length in front of yourself.

"We land at Pontiac airport and it's raining like hell. He's called ahead to have a car waiting for me. I jump out of the plane, into the cab and tell the guy, 'I've got to get to the Silverdome in Pontiac. He said not to worry about traffic and gets me there like 10 minutes before airtime. I go running into the arena, come running down the stairs and there's a wall. The floor was about six feet, maybe more, below the level of seats.

Celtics television broadcasting partners Bob Cousy and Gil Santos. Photo courtesy of Gil Santos

Steve Bulpett of the *Herald* happened to be walking up as I'm throwing the bag over the side. He asked, 'Gil, what are you doing?' I said I just got in from Cincinnati. I've got a raincoat on, I'm all drenched, and I leap over the side. I start running toward the broadcast area and they start the National Anthem. So I stop and I see Cooz down at the broadcast table and he's looking to see if he can find me because he didn't want to go on by himself. He spots me, the Anthem ends and I run like hell over to Cooz and take off my jacket. We stand up, the camera goes on, and I say, 'Good evening everyone!' I made it a minute before tap off!

"The Celtics were a good bunch of guys with coaches KC Jones,

Jimmy Rodgers, and Chris Ford. But Bill Fitch was not a pleasant individual. I managed to get along with him as well as I had to. But the players were good. Kevin McHale and Danny Ainge were real practical jokers and funny guys. Robert Parrish used to like me to tell him jokes because he had a crazy sense of humor. I'd tell him my jokes first because he was such a great audience. People would never have guessed that from what looked like a dour personality, but he was great for jokes—telling them and listening to them. And when you'd tell him one, he'd just go hysterical. Cedric Maxwell was a joy to be with and work around. They were a good bunch of guys and a great, great team. The thing was, no matter where they were playing, there were a tremendous number of Celtic fans. And no matter what the score was, unless it was a 20-point deficit with two minutes left, you always thought the Celtics would win.

"That was especially true with that 1986 team. One night, we were in Cleveland for game three in a best-of-five playoff series. We beat the Cavaliers in Boston the first two games, then went to Cleveland and played in the arena 30 miles out of town—Richland Coliseum. Cooz and I televise game three and we were going to play game four there before coming back to Boston for game five if we lost. So I'm walking with Cooz and Larry Bird to the buses and some fan yells to Bird, 'We're going to beat you tomorrow and we'll see you in Boston for game five!' Larry stops, looks at this guy, and says, 'You've got a better chance of seeing God!'

"It was one of the greatest put down lines I've ever heard!

"Bird used to like to pull practical jokes, too. If our broadcast location was near the Celtics bench—and it was in quite a few arenas, we'd be here, trainer Ray Melchiorre here, and then the coach and players—all in a row with the scorer's table to our right. Many was the time Bird would walk by, I'd have a big cup of soda sitting there and he'd pick it up, take a drink, walk down a few steps, and put it in front of a sportswriter and just go into the game. Or he'd come over to courtside to put the ball in play after a timeout or change of possession and, if he happened to be in front of us and was having a hot night, he'd go 'whew!'—blow on his fingers and he'd smile.

"One time in Portland, we were down by a point with two seconds left. They're going to put the ball in play in front of Cooz and me. As they came walking down, I happened to look up, caught Bird's eye, and he winked and gave me a nod—as if to say, 'Don't worry about a thing.'

They inbound to Bird, he backs up for one dribble, hits the jumper, and they win the game. He was the best player of any team I covered in all my years of broadcasting at the time, rivaled later only by Tom Brady. He was so dominant, so good in the clutch, so confident, and sure of himself. He used to say, 'If we've got the ball and we're down by two points with five seconds left, I think I can win the game.' And he could!"

3

GINO—ANOTHER AMERICAN DREAM

"I gave Gino his start—a five-minute night-time sports program on WCOP radio. I felt he had great potential and I sold the show to Schaefer Beer. This was in the early '60s and Gino got a job on WBZ, so he left WCOP. Gil Santos has a terrific voice, great, knows the game, and the two are very good together."—**FRED CUSICK**, BRUINS HALL OF FAME ANNOUNCER

"Gino is one of the nicest human beings I've ever met. He would never showcase any of his records and achievements. When you hear Gino on the air, he'll never stick it in your face and say 'This is what I've done.' When I was young and green, he was very helpful to me at WRKO. I listen to a lot of Patriots games on radio and I know that when the Patriots get the benefit of a bad call, Gil and Gino will say so. Santos has achieved the full pantheon of legendary status in Boston as did Johnny Most and Bob Wilson—much the same as Ned Martin and Curt Gowdy with the Red Sox."—**JACK EDWARDS**, BRUINS PLAY-CALLER ON NESN

GINO, like his partner Gil Santos, was born a first generation American. He recalled the story of his parents coming to America. "They came from Italy in their early teens back in 1913–15, somewhere in there. They came from two different regions in Italy, but they met in rural Keewatin, Minnesota. A lot of growth in the industry of mining iron ore was taking place in the Mesabi Range and a lot of people coming to this country had some previous relationship with mining and steel-making in Europe. They would come here and then get word back that there was work over here in Minnesota. For example, my father, Mario, told me he'd spent a summer working in the steel mills of Hamburg, Germany even though he was from the outskirts of Milan himself. He may have said something about having experience working in the iron ore mines to someone and was told to go to the Mesabi Range in northern Minnesota in America for work and opportunity.

"The biggest town in that area of Minnesota, locally referred to as the 'Iron Range' or simply 'The Range' is Hibbing. That's where I was born—in Hibbing Hospital, because Keewatin didn't have one. The area is kind of remote, but it's very competitive because the towns were very close—small communities five miles apart, once little mining camps that eventually developed into townships.

"Consequently, it was a great area for sports and little towns competing against one another," Gino recalled. "We were on the borderline of playing 11-man football. Many of the other towns could only support eight-man football teams. I played all the sports: football, basketball, baseball, and track at Keewatin High. I also played Legion Baseball in the summers, and I fought in the Golden Gloves too, but my parents didn't approve of that.

"My school was located within walking distance from our house, I'd say the equivalent of about four city blocks. We would all come out of our houses at the same time and walk to school together. As the seasons changed, the weather changed and you'd see the smoke coming out of chimneys and then the winds would howl. I'm talking about going to school at 30 below and that was before they figured the wind-chill factor.

"I wanted to play football when I was in the eighth grade. That's how small our school was, I was on the team in eighth grade and had to get a permission slip signed by my mother, Rosina, or my father to allow me to play. I went up to my mother and she said, 'No, you go see your father.' He was sitting out in the back of the house by our little garden. We always had a nice little garden that my mother would tend and he would sit by after he came home from working in the mines. I said, 'Pa, I want to play football and I gotta have you sign this card.' He said, 'What-sa this game, Foot-a-ball?' You go have your mother sign it.' So they had me going back and forth. After several rounds of going back and forth between them I stopped halfway and signed it myself. That's how I started playing football. Football was my true love. I really felt an inner passion for it.

"My father used to work in the iron mines. He'd go to work from 7 a.m. to 3:30 in the afternoon and then help my mother with the garden, maybe tend to his wine making, have dinner, go to bed, get up again at five o'clock and off to the mines he'd go again. My brother Guido was much older than me and went off to the war in 1942 in the army, so I really didn't get to know him at a time when brothers might have developed closer bonds. I was just eight or nine years old. He didn't come back until '45 or '46. My sister Carol was older too, so I was kind of an only child in a sense.

"My background was blue-collar, I lived with hard-working people, and the three ethnicities there in Keewatin were Italians, Yugoslavs, and Finns. The rest of the state was Scandinavian and German in the farming areas, but the iron mining attracted the others. So consequently you learned to speak a little bit of all three of those languages to communicate. The first things you learned was how to swear I can cuss in Yugoslav, Finnish, and Italian.

"My father found the time to take me fishing as early as I can remember—in the many lakes of the area. walleye pike was a very desirable fish to get along with bass and muskies. We went hunting too, hunting partridge, rabbits, and deer. I was hunting when I was 12 or 13 years old. Everybody had guns in their houses and they relied on animals for survival and food along with their big beautiful summer gardens. Canning was a big thing to get you through the long winters and if you wanted to keep things cold you just put them out in the porch. We had an old wooden icebox for the summer refrigeration."

A lot of great athletes came out of The Range, the only thing was they had nowhere to go. Nobody knew anything about him or her. A lot of them lacked the schooling and lacked the contacts to have anybody see them play or perform to offer any scholarship help. So a lot of the kids just wound up working in the mines the rest of their lives. It was at that time, the 1940s when the war was on and a lot of the guys went to war which broke up their high school athletic careers if they were going to have one. There was just no exposure, no scouts, no one would be up in The Range. Duluth was the nearest big city and was 60 miles away. Hibbing of course was next door.

"Hibbing did have some famous people come out of it in the 1960s. Vincent Bugliosi was the prosecutor of the Charles Manson murder case. Bobby Dylan is from Hibbing. His real name was Bobby Zimmerman. His family had a bakery in Hibbing and they moved to Duluth after a few years. Kevin McHale is another great athlete who came from Hibbing. Roger Maris was born in Hibbing. His real name was Maras. His father and father's brother had a bar. They got into an argument about the bar one day and had a falling out. Roger's father was so upset with his brother and the rest of his family that he took his own family and went to Fargo, North Dakota and changed his name to Maris."

Hunting, fishing, trapping, and sports of all kinds provided all the recreation a kid could want in the rural Minnesota of Gino's youth. Gino found his natural athleticism combined with the cultural importance of sports in the area allowed him to be successful in almost anything he tried from the start. Almost anything.

"When I went into my first boxing match for the golden gloves it was with a guy named Eugene Rivers who had just come out of the Navy. He was 21 and I was 14 or 15. I came out like a whirlwind. Nothing happened. He didn't go down, he didn't get hurt, and eventually he was able to beat me. But boxing was pretty big up on the Iron Range and I took to it until my parents asked me to quit. My father asked me to quit. I said, 'Pa, all right but let me win a fight first and then I'll quit. He said, 'No! That might take too long!' I think he was just kidding, but I did quit. I played hockey as well. We had outdoor rinks and people would stand up on the snow banks to watch. Then basketball grabbed my fancy and I played that. You couldn't play both hockey and basketball because they were both winter sports.

"Football was my first love; it seems to have been inbred in me. I have pictures of me at five years of age with a football under my arm. I took it to bed with me. Football was the outlet that we all had as kids up on The Range.

"Once the tomatoes were done and gone in the gardens around Keewatin, we would go in them to play because it was soft dirt and we could tackle and fall without too much damage. We used to come out of those games looking like you couldn't imagine—covered with dirt and squashed tomatoes and whatever other vegetable matter was left on the

Five-year-old Gino Cappelletti with his beloved football playing on his front lawn in Keewatin. Photo courtesy of Gino Cappelletti

ground. In the wintertime, we used to play football in the plowed streets and push each other into the snow banks.

"I always wanted to be the kicker. I had the natural ability to kick. I would kick the ball at telephone poles for a goal post. You would dig a hole in the dirt with your heel to hold it upright then kick it and try to hit he pole. Punting was more fun. Every kid likes to try and get the ball to spiral off your foot. But kicking was just something I could do. I was able to lock my ankle down and go after the ball, so it was a gift. All of the kids who tried kicking would try to get hold of their father's steel-toed mining boots to kick with. If you were lucky and your father had small feet or you had big feet, you were in luck.

"One time in the fall, I was playing football with my friends in the street outside my house when I saw the grape truck coming and I knew what that meant. Sometimes I'd pretend I didn't see it. My father came out and gave me *the whistle*. That whistle was very distinct. It meant that I had to come home whenever I heard him whistle. This time I had to go and help unload the grapes down into the basement. Then I had to get ready to start stomping. My father had a bad hip and I was the one who had to stomp the grapes to make the wine. One time I was slow answering the whistle, so he came over to my game and disrupted it in a hurry as he dragged me by my ear and said, 'Did you hear me?' So from then on I always answered his whistle.

"My father had these white knee-length rubber boots that he would scrub first and then I put them on. They were much too big, but it gave me more mashing power as I would stomp the grapes in his big washtub. We made zinfandel and muscatel from the tub, to the press, to the barrels." Gino suggested half jokingly that perhaps his strong kicking legs may have been developed as a result of the many times he squashed the grapes to make the wine.

Gino brought his gifted kicking toe and his athletic ability to Keewatin High School and in his freshman, junior, and senior years, Keewatin won league championships. "We were the only high school in our league that kicked for extra points. I was able to consistently kickoff into the opposition's end zone from our 40. That was not common."

Gino was named as an all-star halfback in all of those seasons and in his senior year he was named to the Minnesota all-state football team—something unheard of for a kid from tiny Keewatin! "For me to make all-state meant that somebody was following my career. Hibbing had a coach who played at the University of Minnesota. There was another

The 1950 Keewatin High School backfield. (Left to right) Gino Cappelletti, Pat Adams, Dan Kukich, and Gene Cortese. Photo courtesy of Gino Cappelletti

fellow in my hometown, Vic Spadacinni, who played at the university at one time before the war that could have had some influence. John Mariucci was a hockey star at the university. Mariucci was the first American-born player in the National Hockey league, playing for the Chicago Blackhawks. He was from the Range town of Eveleth—about 20 miles from Keewatin. He was another influential person that may have put the word in for me. So, I was offered a scholarship at Minnesota. I had a feeler from Notre Dame and one from Southern Cal but they were just feelers. We were so remote up there that there was hardly any national scouting of any sort going on. I thought the University of Minnesota would be the best place. It was three hours from home driving, so that's where I went."

Gino credits his hometown community and its work ethic with preparing him in many ways for a college football career. "In my day, there was no weight-lifting or training like there is today. We all just worked hard to be in shape. My first job was setting pins at the local bowling alley when I was 12. The next job was working on the railroad that serviced the mining industry. That is where I think I really developed physically when I was 15 and 16. Lifting rails, lifting ties, working from eight to five all summer long. Then, when you were 17, you could work in the mines—in the pits, driving trucks, pulling cables, whatever they needed for labor. So my senior year in high school I was able to work the mines and also during the first three years in college when I came home to work."

The University of Minnesota provided Gino with an opportunity to take his considerable athletic abilities to a higher level and he played both offense and defense for the Golden Gophers. "That was a time when the game called for it—before they went to two-platoon. I had good instincts, a good feel for the game. My most natural position was halfback. Running the ball in high school and college showed that was my key position, though I could play defense as well and was a cornerback.

Gino was a skilled running back as well as a defensive standout at the University of Minnesota, but a switch to quarterback gave him more playing time. Photo courtesy of Gino Cappelletti

"Our coach Wes Fesler, said, 'I'd like to get you into the lineup more, but you're behind an All-American, Paul Giel, at halfback so do you want to try quarterback?' I said sure, so I became the quarterback as a sophomore and stayed there as a junior and senior. But it was a different type of quarterback. We played split-T, single-wing and I also played defense and kicked extra points. But field goals were a rarity during the 1950s. I only attempted one and that was against Iowa in our Homecoming game."

That kick was a story in itself, and the beginning of kicking greatness to come with the Patriots. "I don't know what lifted me. I was just playing on defense as a sophomore at the time, but I got up off the bench during that game against Iowa, went up to Fesler on the sideline and said, 'Coach, if we don't make this third down, you want me to try a field goal?' He looked at me and said, 'Go back and sit down!' Well, we didn't make the third down, so he turned around, looked at me and said, 'Come here! Go in and kick that thing!' The score was tied, 7–7, and the kick was 40-some yards. I came out on the field and said, 'I'm gonna kick a field goal.' The guys in the huddle were looking at me as if to say,

'What do you mean a field goal?' I said, like an extra point the quarterback was going to hold. I nailed it and we took the lead and eventually won the game 17–7!

"So afterward, Fesler—a dynamic guy who'd coached at Ohio State—made a big thing of it. He said kind of excitedly and proudly to the press, 'The kid came up and asked if I wanted him to kick a field goal.' I guess it was a big deal because field goal kicking was pretty rare in college football then."

At Minnesota in 1952–54, Cappelletti, nicknamed the "Keewatin Kid," by the legendary Golden Gopher broadcaster Halsey Hall, played well enough to be considered for All-Big 10 honorable mention. He booted that 47-yard field goal against Iowa in 1952, and over the course of his three varsity seasons he made 48 PATs and scored six touchdowns. After Minnesota, Gino went up to Canada and played semi-professional football in the Ontario Ruby Football Union. The following year, Gino tried out unsuccessfully with the Detroit Lions in the NFL, was released, and soon after was drafted into the US Army. He served at Ft. Sill, Oklahoma, where he received All-Army and All-Service recognition in 1957 playing in the military football league. "Then I went back up to Canada during the season after I got out of the service and finished off the year playing there.

Known as the "Keewatin Kid" to Big-10 fans, Gino shows his form as a kicker for the Golden Gophers of Minnesota. Photo courtesy of Gino Cappelletti

"After that I went to work at a bar—Mac's and Cap's—which my brother Guido and Bob McNamara owned near the University of Minnesota campus. Bob was an All-American halfback and my teammate in college. To this day he is still a dear friend of mine. My appetite for football continued but I had to resort to *touch* football in the Minneapolis Park Board league, representing Mac's and Cap's!"

During the winter of 1959

there was talk about a new pro football league, which caught the attention of Gino. Having played some defense at Minnesota, Gino thought that might be his best shot for a chance in the NFL or the new league he had heard about that was getting a lot of attention—the American Football League. But he had to sell himself. "The pros didn't come looking for me, so I called up Lou Saban, the Patriots' first coach, and asked for a tryout. He asked what position I played and I said defensive back. That was because I had tried out as a quarterback with the Detroit and just didn't have it. I was there one week and they let me go. Defense wasn't my real position, but I thought I might have a better chance

In 1960 Gino found his path to professional football in the new American Football League with the Boston Patriots. He became a two-way star as a receiver (right) and as a kicker (below). Gino set numerous scoring records over his 11-year pro career. Photos courtesy of Gino Cappelletti

catching on that way. I also used to catch some balls as a quarterback at Minnesota going out in the single wing, so I was willing to try anything.

"It was 1960 and I wanted to stay on a team long enough for the coaches to see me kick. So with the Patriots, trying out as a defensive back, I hit anything and everything that moved, piled on, and did anything to make myself visible—just so I could hang around so they could see me kick. Finally, after about two weeks of that, we had our first intrasquad game. Saban had to get somebody to kick. He said anybody who wanted to be looked at, as a kicker, should come out before practice at 8 a.m. So I went out, started kicking, and won the job. I liked Lou, he was a tough hombre, and I could see why he was a good football player—a linebacker for the Cleveland Browns. He was tough, wanted to talk tough, and wanted *you* to be tough. He was very straightforward with me."

Cappelletti was the new guy on a brand new team in a brand new league—the American Football League. The AFL was a league that was to revolutionize professional football with its wide-open passing game and excitement that was just right for television. The AFL also brought professional football to many cities from coast to coast that were not being served by the established thirteen-team National Football League—cities like Buffalo, Houston, Dallas, Denver, and Oakland. Boston was another one of those cities; the Boston Patriots was its team. Sports fans in Boston would see their new professional football team play in four temporary homes—Boston University Field, Harvard Stadium, Boston College, and at Fenway Park—as the team set its roots in New England during its early years.

Lamar Hunt, just 26 years old and from Dallas, was the primary founder and force behind the establishment of the AFL. The original eight-team league consisted of the Patriots, Buffalo Bills, Houston Oilers, New York Titans, Dallas Texans (the NFL also established the expansion Cowboys in Dallas in 1960, some say to try to thwart Hunt's new league), Denver Broncos, Oakland Raiders, and the Los Angeles Chargers. In 1963 the Chargers relocated to San Diego, with the Miami Dolphins and the Cincinnati Bengals added in 1966 and 1968 expansions.

Today the American Football Conference Championship trophy—a piece of hardware the Patriots have won six times since the AFL-NFL merger in 1970—bears Hunt's name. Cappelletti holds a special place for Lamar Hunt in his heart. "I had a very nice relationship with Lamar, who died in December of 2006," Gino declared. "When I was in his

Fenway Park configured for football. Note the stands set up in front of the "Green Monster" and the "H" style goalposts. The Patriots played in Fenway from 1963–68 and compiled a record of 17–16–5 (.513) during their tenancy there. Photo courtesy of Gino Cappelletti

company, I made sure I told him how grateful I was for the courage he showed in starting the AFL. What's happened in my life and in the lives of the other AFL players, and whatever benefits have come our way, are due to his founding the league.

"When the Patriots played Kansas City over the last 10 years, he'd come to our broadcast booth to see me. He had an apartment at the stadium there and I was invited there. The last time we were in Kansas City, he came to the booth and a funny thing happened. Marc Cappello, the producer of our radio broadcasts for WBCN, tapped me on the shoulder and said, 'Lamar Hunt's here. He wants to see you!' I turned and joked, 'Tell him I'm busy!' And Mark said, 'Are you crazy?' 'No,' I said seriously this time, 'just forever grateful.'"

Cappelletti came to the Patriots as a free agent on June 23, 1960 at age 26 as a 6-foot, 190-pound quarterback from the University of Minnesota. One of the original Patriots, known to his teammates as the "Duke," Gino was so successful in his 11-year career with the team that he is now known by most fans simply as "Mr. Patriot." As a starting defensive back in 1960, the Pats' first season, he made three interceptions in one game against Oakland and had four that season, for 68 yards. At the suggestion of coach Mike Holovak, "They also had me working as a split end on offense," Gino said.

As to how he became known as "Duke," Gino had this explanation: "There are two reasons why I think I got the nickname here in Boston right away. I was getting on a plane and I had a gold jacket on and tan slacks, or something like that. Harry Jagielski, a defensive tackle from Indiana University, was sitting with Walter Cudzik, our center from Purdue. Of course I was from Minnesota—the Big 10. I don't know if the rivalries between the schools tied into it, but there was always a lot of joking around between guys who played for different college teams or in different conferences.

"So, as I walked on the plane Harry was sitting up front and said 'Lookie, lookie, lookie, here comes a symphony in gold...the Duke himself!' That kind of got it started verbally. The other thing was that I used to have a habit when we used to go out. We always had a gang who liked to go out and have dinner, drinks, and fun in the early years. I would always say to the other guys, 'Look it, you duke [or dook] the maître d', you duke the valet, I'll take care of this, or something like that. I was using the expression to mean tipping. And that basically was it, the guys started calling me the Duke—and the nickname stuck.

"It's amazing how there is a certain crowd that called me Duke and other ones who call me Gino. I associate different people with one name or the other."

In the late summer of 1960, the Patriots were practicing for their first exhibition game as Chubby Checker was debuting his new hit song, "The Twist" on Dick Clark's *American Bandstand* show. The *Flintstones* premiered as the first cartoon show shown on primetime television and Eisenhower was still in the Oval Office. The first Nixon-Kennedy televised debate aired across the nation that summer as well. It was a time of innovations, new ideas, and promise in America—from the silly to the serious. The time was perfect for the arrival of the new American Football League. Skeptics however, wondered if the venture was a silly or a serious one at the time. But the league eventually took root and soon would force the hand of the senior National Football League to recognize it and eventually merge with the upstart eight-team league.

"Our first exhibition game was in Buffalo at War Memorial Stadium.

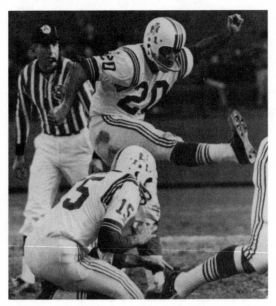

Gino shown kicking a record setting 53-yard field goal against the New York Jets in 1965, the Pats won 27–23, and Ginos' record held up for 35 years until Adam Vinatieri booted a 54-yarder in 2001. The referee seen in the photo is Ben Dreith, infamous to Patriots fans later on because of a highly questionable roughing the passer penalty call against Ray "Sugar Bear" Hamilton in a 1976 AFC playoff game vs. the Oakland Raiders. The call set up a game-winning touchdown for Oakland (24–21) with seconds left on the clock. Photo courtesy of Gino Cappelletti

We won, 28–7 and then we beat Denver in Providence, 44–6. The Broncos stayed in Providence for our home opener the next week and upset us, 13–10 at Nickerson Field in Boston—Boston University Field," recalled Cappelletti, "we started on a Friday night—September 9, 1960—and the rest of the league didn't open until that Sunday afternoon. I was disappointed with the loss, however I kicked one of the most important field goals of my career because if I missed, then coach Lou Saban was sure to replace me with another kicker on the next try."

It was also a very important kick in football history, as Gino's first three career points were the very first points scored in the American Football League, and in the history of the Patriots.

"We played a lot of Friday night games at home during the first two seasons as Billy Sullivan didn't want to go head to head with the Giants NFL broadcast at 1 p.m. every Sunday. We did play on Sundays when were on the road. There was no national television contract so each team had local television deals. Some cities, like Denver, didn't have any NFL competition so Sundays were OK for them to play without any competition. When the AFL finally got a national TV contract, in 1963 or 1964, they were pretty clever in scheduling the games on national television for four o'clock on Sunday afternoons. The football fans could watch the

NFL at one, then with their appetites whet for more football, the AFL came on at four."

Billy Sullivan needed to save money in operational expenses for the new Patriots team. After the league had been in existence for a couple of years and rivalries began to establish themselves, Sullivan and Buffalo owner Ralph Wilson got together on a plan to cut down on transportation costs. Both the Bills and the Patriots were scheduled to play on the west coast during the same week. Boston was playing at Denver and the Bills were in Oakland for the first game of a two-week stay in California. The following weekend they would play in San Diego. The two owners of the rival teams hatched a plan to *share* the same charter flight out west. The plane took off from Boston then went to Buffalo to pick up the Bills. Gino Cappelletti was on the flight and recalled, "All of the Boston players, who got on the plane first, naturally took all the good seats. They filled up the first class section and got the best of the rest according to their likes. Well, when we landed in Buffalo, the Bills players were miffed. Back in those days we really didn't socialize with the players on other teams like you see today. They were bitter rivals. We landed in Denver and the Patriots got off as the charter continued to Oakland. Because the Bills had a game in San Diego the next week we did not fly back together, thank goodness. That was the last of the scheme to have two teams double up on a flight."

The first year Patriots finished with just five wins against nine losses but things turned around the next year. In 1961, when he began to primarily play offense as a flanker-back (receiver) and was the team's place-kicker, Cappelletti became the American Football League record-setting scorer with 147 points—eight touchdowns, 48 points after touchdowns, and 17 field goals (which led the league in that department as well). Mike Holovak, who became head coach five games into the season, had urged Gino to switch from defensive back to offensive receiver. Gino has said often that 1961 was his "break-out year" as a pro football player.

The story of Gino's success in professional football is an inspiring one. Once fighting for a chance to play on a professional football team, he was now one of the biggest stars in the new American Football League. He was an offensive standout, was the Pats' placekicking specialist, and he still even played a little on defense as the team's sixth and last defensive back. His most dramatic field goal was a 28-yard boot on the final play of an 18–17 win in Dallas. The Pats had been down, 17–7. With the game televised back to Boston, Gino's dramatic kick established the Pats as an institution in the eyes of New England fans. Gino was the Pats' Most Valuable Player and was runner-up to George Blanda of the champion Houston Oilers for American Football League MVP. The franchise finished in second place in the AFC Eastern division with a 9–4–1 record for 1961.

In 1962, Gino married Sandra Sadowsky of Framingham on July 29. They resided in Wellesley, where they still live. Gino had another sensational year on the field as he tied Abner Haynes as the league's second best scorer with 128 points. Gino regained the AFL scoring title the next year with 113 points and in the 1963 postseason, added four field goals and two point after touchdowns in the Patriots' 26–8 playoff victory for the Eastern Division title at Buffalo. Gino had kicked 72 field goals so far in his four-year career. The Patriots had another strong season at 9–4–1 and were drawing the fans into their rented home field at Boston University. The Academy of Sports Editors voted Gino the AFL Eastern Division's outstanding player. He also starred in the league All-Star Game in San Diego.

Through 1963, Gino gained the equivalent of *over a mile* in offensive yardage in his Pats' career. His pass catching was the second best on the team with 35 catches for 493 yards for the 7–6–1 Patriots. In addition to enjoying a great football career, Gino became a dad when the Cappellettis had a baby daughter, Gina Rose, born in December.

Quarterback Babe Parilli, Gino, and running back Ron Burton celebrating the Patriots first-ever playoff victory, a 26–8 win at Buffalo, for the AFL Eastern Division title. Photo courtesy of Gino Cappelletti

Gino swept every poll as the American Football League's Most Valuable Player and broke his own AFL scoring record with 155 points in 1964—seven touchdowns, a perfect 36-for-36 on point afters, and he kicked 25 field goals. He even added a two-point conversion to his 1964 point total. His AFL mark of 155 points in one season was the second best in pro football history at the time, topped only by Paul Hornung's 176 points scored in the National Football League in 1960. Today, 44 years later, Gino's record still ranks fourth in NFL history. He also set an *all-time* professional football record with six field goals in one game—a 39–10 victory October 4, 1964 at Denver.

"Bob Waterfield, who was married to actress Jane Russell, had the longtime record of five in a game and I always was aware of it," recalled Gino. "I had kicked four field goals a few times and I always knew Waterfield, a quarterback and a kicker, had that record of five field goals when he kicked for the Los Angeles Rams in the 1950s." said Gino. The victory at Denver was a big one. It capped a season-opening four-game winning streak and the Patriots finished the year with a 10–3–1 record—their best ever so far, but they still had to settle for second place in the AFC East.

Cappelletti was on a pace that would see him go on to become the AFL's all-time career scoring leader with 1,130 points.

His most important single contribution to the 1964 season was a last-second 41-yard field goal, his fourth of the game, which beat Houston, 25–24, November 6 at Fenway Park. He was mobbed by fans, needed a police escort out of the park, and was named AFL player of the week. One of the highlights for Gino that season was scoring 24 points, including three touchdowns, in a game against archrival Buffalo which ended a Bills' nine-game win streak. He led all Pats' receivers for the year with 49 catches for 851 yards and an impressive 17.3 yards-per-catch average.

By 1964, thanks to more and more exposure on television, now beaming the games into American homes in "Living Color," pro athletes were beginning to acquire celebrity status beyond their exploits on football fields, baseball diamonds, and basketball courts.

Boston Red Sox star reliever Dick "The Monster" Radatz was one of Boston's first sports stars to try his hand in broadcasting. Legendary announcer Fred Cusick had encouraged Radatz, a most affable individual despite his intimidating nickname, to try announcing sports on Boston AM radio station WCOP. Every morning during the Red Sox season when the Sox were in town, Radatz would do the morning sports on WCOP out of the transmitting facilities in Waltham, Massachusetts. Dick did what was called a rip and read. He would get the latest scores and sports stories off of the station's newswire machine (rip) and then broadcast the information (read) after the station's other morning men delivered the news and weather.

One day Gino ran into Radatz at a social occasion and learned that he was planning to return to his native Michigan after the 1964 Red Sox season. Radatz suggested that Gino consider picking up the radio job when he left. Gino remembered his sudden introduction to broadcasting. "Well, the very next day I got a call from Fred Cusick who said, 'Gino, how about I pick you up tomorrow at about 5:30 a.m.? I'll bring you to the station to watch what Dick does and maybe you can give it a try.' So, the next day I went into the studio and tried it myself. I read some scores—live and on the air. It was my audition right there and then. The station manager, John Crohan, came up to me and said, "You want the job? You want it, you got it." And that was that.

"So I would be up at 5 a.m., drive to Waltham and be on the air at six.

Patriots' president Billy Sullivan looks on as Gino signs his first television contact with WBZ. Also pictures are newsman Gene Pell (standing, center) and WBZ general manager Lamont Thompson (standing, right). *Boston Herald* photo

At 8:30 I'd get over to Route 2 to drive into practice everyday at East Boston Stadium by the airport in East Boston. After a while they moved the studio into Copley Square and I worked from there.

"In 1965 I received a telegram from WBZ Television—that is how they did things in those days, they sent me a telegram—saying that they wanted to talk with me about doing some sports on TV with them. Dick Stuart of the Red Sox was doing the sports reports at night for them at the time.

"They hired me to do the sports segment of the 11 o'clock news. Billy Sullivan held a press conference to announce the news that I was going to be on WBZ-TV. Mr. Sullivan especially liked the exposure it got the Patriots. I did it for a year, but after a while I found it to be very taxing trying to play football and keep up that schedule."

In 1964 Gino was a bona fide professional football star, shown here returning to the locker room after a pre-game warm-up at Fenway Park. *Boston Herald* photo

Gino was considered the AFL's best all-around player in 1965. He led the Patriots with 37 catches and was the AFL scoring champion for the fourth year. He set a Pats field goal record with a 53-yard kick against the Jets and also set a single-game scoring record with 28 points in the season finale. Through the 1965 season, he had a career 200 catches for 3,299 yards, 31 touchdowns, and 109 field goals. However, the Pats finished the year third in the AFC East with a disappointing 4–8–2 record, under fifth-year head coach Mike Holovak.

One of the keys to Cappelletti's success on the field was the preparation and thought he gave to improving his game off the field. Long before sports psychology and mental preparedness came in vogue, Gino would imagine and prepare for whatever bounce the ball might take in a game. "I had thought about many game situations at night lying in bed

Gino was named the American Football league's most Valuable Player in 1964. Gino is shown here at the 1964 AFL all-star game with (left to right) Barron Hilton, owner of the San Diego Chargers, Tobin Rote, quarterback of the Chargers, and the 1963 AFL MVP, Joe Foss, the commissioner of the AFL, Gino, and Billy Sullivan, president of the Boston Patriots Football Club. Photo courtesy of Gino Cappelletti

and rehearsed in my mind what I might do, or what I should do in an unusual circumstance—and it paid off.

"For example in a situation where you see everybody react in a certain way over and over and you think well maybe something else would be the better thing to do. Sure enough that happened to me in a game and I reacted instantly because I had kind of visualized the situation in my head. One night, lying in bed reflecting, I was thinking about what would happen during a field goal attempt, especially a long one, if they snapped the ball over my head. What would I do? Usually everybody runs back and tries to pick the ball up for a pass, which doesn't usually work out. I thought that's not the thing to do. It's fourth down anyway, I thought the right thing to do would be to pick the ball up and punt it!

[The most infamous example of a kicker-turned passer in desperation was Miami kicker Gary Yepremian whose pass of a loose ball was intercepted by Mike Bass of the Redskins who ran it back for a TD in the 1973 Super Bowl!]

"I was in the All-Star game in San Diego and that exact situation happened. Babe (Parilli) who was also on the team with me was down on his knee to hold. The ball sailed over his head on the snap so I ran back, got the ball, and *punted* it. It got downed inside the 10-yard line. So that was great. If you missed a field goal then it was placed on the 20. If I threw it and it was incomplete, the other side would have taken the ball at the original line of scrimmage. So the punt played a little part in the game, which we won.

"Sid Gilman was the coach and said afterwards to me, 'Well, Gino that was some quick thinking.' But it really was something I had already thought about a lot should it ever happen, and it did."

Gino was an AFL all-star once again and the AFL scoring champion for a fifth year in 1966. Since becoming a Patriot, Gino had played in every game. Again not missing a game in the 1966 season, he caught 43 passes, scored six touchdowns, and scored 119 points. As football's best all-around player, he also lengthened his lead in the AFL's lifetime scoring list with 854 points. The season saw a great improvement for the team as well, as Holovak and the Pats turned things around to finish 8–4–2 for second place in the AFC East. The off season proved even better for Gino and his wife Sandy as the Cappellettis' second daughter, Cara Mia, was born February 23, 1967.

Meanwhile, Gino was showing the public some of his business skills in the fall of 1967 when he and several other investors opened up a popular restaurant and club aptly named The Point After. "I used to go into this place called the Darbury Lounge on Dartmouth Street in the Back Bay when I first came to Boston. I was living nearby at the Vendome Hotel

Gino and friends celebrate the opening night at The Point After. (Left to right) Babe Parilli, Jim Colclough, Gino, and Joe Namath. Photo courtesy of Gino Cappelletti

at the time. I moved in there with several other Patriot players. I guess we all preferred hotels because we wanted to see if the team was going to make it, if the league was going to make it. It didn't seem to make sense to lease a house in those days. So, three of us rented a suite on Dartmouth, near Copley Square and we frequented the Darbury on occasion. I had gotten to know the manager Saul 'Patch' Sussman pretty well, and a few years later he told

Billy Sullivan, Gino, and Sandy Cappelletti celebrate Gino's 1,000th point for the Patriots. Gino was the first AFL player ever to reach that lofty goal, and Gino's career point total of 1,130 remains the AFL record (set during 14-game seasons not the current 16) and places Gino near the top 20 all-time point scorers in all of pro football. It should be noted that Gino's 7.48 points per game average remains the highest in pro football history. Hall of Fame running back Paul Horning of Green Bay follows Gino on that exclusive list. *Boston Herald* photo

me that the owner was looking to get out of the business and that he would be interested in running it. I said that I might be interested in investing and to make a long story short, through him and few other investors we went in to buy the place. I had the idea to call it The Point After and the partners wanted me to be the front man anyway. We made it a restaurant, not a sports bar, with live music but gave it a sports atmosphere. We had goal posts out in front. It was a place everyone enjoyed and felt comfortable in."

Through 1967, Gino had a lifetime total of 278 catches, 40 touchdowns, 125 field goals, and 278 point after touchdowns. In 1968, Gino became the first American Football League player to eclipse 1,000 points with 1,032. He was fifth among active AFL receivers with 291 catches for 4,568 yards and had not missed a game in nine years. Gino led the Pats in scoring once again and was named to the AFC All-Star team for the fifth time. The team struggled with a 4–10 record and the loyal hometown fans only saw two victories at Fenway Park that year.

Nineteen sixty-eight would be coach Mike Holovak's eighth and final season at the helm. In 1969, Clive Rush was named the Patriots' new

Gino and his family enjoy a Christmas at home together. Soon Gino would be retiring from football and would begin a career in broadcasting. From left: Sandy, Gino's mother Rosina, Gino holding Cara Mia, Gino's father Mario, and Gina Rose. Photo courtesy of Gino Cappelletti

Anxious to keep the public interested in the team and into the stands at Harvard Stadium— Pats' the fourth leased home in 10 years— the Patriots publicity department may have dreamed up this photo opportunity to attract some attention. Actress/dancer/singing star Joey Heatherton paid a visit to the Patriots' practice facility and posed holding the ball for Gino in this shot. Photo courtesy of Gino Cappelletti

head coach—the third since 1960. Rush announced that Gino would be co-captain of the Patriots along with six-time AFL All-Star defensive tackle Houston Antoine. Gino added punting and kickoffs to his repertoire. At season's end, Gino remained the AFL's active scoring leader but the team again had a disappointing year, finishing at just 4–10 once again.

By 1970 it was clear that the Patriots organization was in a funk. Mike Holovak's last two years, 1967 and 1968, saw the team finish with records of 3–10–1, and 4–10. Clive Rush represented new coaching blood but he also only managed a 4–10 record in his first season. More than change in coaching was needed. Changes on the field—new players—were inevitable. Veteran Vikings quarterback Joe Kapp was brought in as a stopgap measure to put some fans back in the seats, but his presence in a Patriots uniform was not enough to stem the tide of Patriots losses and Joe's single year with the Pats proved to be his swansong.

It was clear that the Patriots were in for plenty of changes. The ownership had to rebuild, and even replaced new head coach Rush midway through the 1970 season with John Mazur, who in turn only lasted another full season before he was also sacked mid-year in 1972.

Things were not good for the itinerant Patriots franchise in 1970, a season that saw them playing in their fourth and final rented facility, Harvard Stadium. They won just two games while losing a dozen. It was the worst season ever in the 11-year history of the club. Most of the players who were members of the original 1960 team were gone and Gino decided to retire at the end of the season. He was ready for some new challenges after a playing career where he led the AFL in scoring five times before the NFL merger. His team may have won only two games in his last season, but he left as the third leading scorer in *pro football* history.

After 11 years as an active player in professional football, Gino considered many career opportunities. He was pleased to find an outlet for his talents, keeping him close to the game he loved as a five-year-old kid in Keewatin who took a football to bed.

Gino built upon his previous seasonal and part-time sports reporting experience and applied his talents full time. He became one of the first and most successful ex-players to find he had an aptitude behind the microphone as a football announcer and commentator. Gino Cappelletti would go on to spend the next three decades as one of America's most knowledgeable and respected college and professional football broadcasters.

4
PARTNERS

"Gil and Gino are not only a terrific team, they're a big part of the Patriots fabric. They work so well together. Gil is one of the best play-by-play men going. I'm a big fan. He's outstanding and very accurate. Gino? He's one of those certain legendary characters who are involved with their team over a long period. He's loyal to the Patriots and very good on game analysis."—**JERRY TRUPIANO**, RED SOX RADIO VOICE OF 14 YEARS (1993–2006)

GINO CAPPELLETTI AND GIL SANTOS first met in 1966 when Gil began calling Patriots games at Fenway Park and when WBZ first was awarded the radio contract. Santos and Bob Starr did the broadcasts, taking over from the WEEI announcing team of Ned Martin and Fred Cusick (from 1960 to 1964 Bob Gallagher and Cusick sat behind the WEEI Patriots' mikes).

Gino, the Patriots' foremost star, was setting scoring records in the American Football League as the league's premier place-kicker and as an all-star wide receiver at the time. After five appearances in the AFL All-Star Game, and after setting the Patriots all-time scoring record of 1,130 points over his 11-year career, a record that held until 2005 when place-kicker Adam Vinatieri reached 1,158. It should also be noted that Gino's record was set during an era of a 14 game schedule, as opposed to the 16 game schedule adopted by the NFL in 1978. Gino retired as a player after the 1970 season, opening the door to numerous post-football career options.

In 1972, WBZ station executives wanted to add a new element of insight and credibility to the broadcasts by including a former player on their broadcast team. That is when relatively recently retired Cappelletti had his opportunity. The station conducted extensive tryouts via simulated games, working off a television tape of a game with Gil doing the play-by-play and the candidate analyzing the action. A number of top candidates applied for the spot, including Jim Nance and Upton Bell. "Nance was pretty good, but Gino was far and away the top candidate,"

Santos recalled. "He was the guy. And we hit it off. There was an instant rapport, a real chemistry that I could feel right away. We were friendly and came in with the same type of background.

"Gino seemed eager and willing to learn the broadcast business and he understood when I said, 'Don't feel you have to say something after every play.' And he didn't. The reason I said that, and explained to him, is there are guys who do color, former players, who feel to justify their position, they have to say something after every play. When you get 150 plays in a football game, he says 150 things and only 50 percent of them are good or add to the broadcast, which means he said 75 things that were meaningless. So what I urged him to do was, say what you feel, what you see. Why did something work? Why did something not work? And when you feel it, you say it. If you don't feel it, don't say it. That way, if you only say something every other play and you only say 75 things, then you'll probably get 75 percent of those that are good. So your percentage of saying things that are meaningful in the game is much higher. And the broadcast is not cluttered. That year was our first with the Patriots and we've been going at it ever since with various calls—the Patriots, Boston College, the Boston Breakers. Gino even helped me work some Boston Marathons."

Gino recalled that his new position, combined with his previous broadcasting experiences on WCOP and as the evening sportscaster on WBZ-TV, provided him with many additional and interesting professional and community service opportunities. Gino's celebrity and popularity as an announcer grew in the 1970s and he was asked to contribute his talents to the annual Boston Youth Concert at Symphony Hall, working alongside famed conductor Harry Ellis Dickson. Gino was asked to narrate the story of "Freddie the Football" for an assembled young audience, and the Boston Symphony Orchestra accompanied his reading. Freddie was a forlorn little football sitting by himself on a sporting goods store shelf. Freddie bemoaned the fact that all of his friends—the other sports balls were being bought and played with while he remained tucked away gathering dust. The story concluded happily when Freddie was chosen as the ball for the Super Bowl and presumably lived happily ever after.

That debut with the Boston Symphony led to an appearance with the Boston Ballet Company where Gino narrated the well-known story of "Peter and the Wolf." Later he encored his recitation of "Freddie the Football," this time for an adult audience, at the Boston Pops with

Boston Symphony Orchestra conductor Harry Ellis Dickson and several young audience members at a rehearsal of "Freddie the Football" narrated by Gino. Photo courtesy of Gino Cappelletti

Arthur Fiedler conducting. During the Bicentennial celebration events of 1976, at the historic Old North Church, Gino did a reading of Paul Revere's own account of his famous ride of April 18, 1775. President Gerald Ford was the guest of honor at the event and Senator Edward W. Brooke shared the dais with Gino and the President. Gino's many civic contributions and theatrical appearances during the years immediately following his football career accelerated his transition from a football hero to a well-respected broadcast personality.

As much as he was enjoying his association with the performing arts and doing community service events, Gino's first love was football broadcasting. Gino recalled his first game teamed with Gil. Santos was of course the play-by play announcer and Gino was cast with him as the expert game analyst, or commentator, or color man.

"Take your pick of titles," Gino will joke today. "My first game behind the mike was an exhibition game at Oakland in 1972. I'm a little concerned, a little uptight. So we go up to the Coliseum and lo and behold, we were sitting in the stadium's *seats*! There was no broadcast booth! They put a plank on top of the row of seats in front of us and that was our desk with a couple of microphones and fans sitting behind us, beside us, and in front of us—we were sitting right in with the crowd! Here I've got my paperwork, Gil's got his stuff, and all we've got is a plank of wood.

So I asked Gil, 'So this is the big time? This is the way it is, huh?' It was quite an introduction to this job. Fans were hollering and standing up in front of us. To start with, that made it a difficult broadcast for me. It was live, the baseball season was still on, and much of the play was on the dirt of the baseball diamond. They didn't have the field laid out like they normally would by taking seats out. They just laid it out in a fashion that would conform to the diamond, just taking the baseball lines out. That's why we sat where we did. Otherwise, we'd have been in the corner of the end zone."

Gil had similar recollections of that first game with Gino. "Gino's buddies had sent him a big good-luck horseshoe-shaped wreath, like they give to a horse in the winner's circle! But this one had a distinctly *Italian* theme to it—just for Gino. It was a big flowered thing and it was also filled with garlic and peppers!

"That game ended and we're getting our gear together to go back out to the plane. He said, 'I have a new appreciation for what you try to do.' He had no idea what went into it. At that time, I did my own producing and used a stopwatch. I'd take a break, time it out to 65 seconds and you go back on the air. It's all very precise and I had to do all that myself. It wasn't like now when we have a producer on site with us whether we're home or on the road."

Some primitive conditions might have been expected in the early years of the American Football League—certainly with all of the temporary and older stadiums used in those years. But even today, Gil and Gino are thrust into some difficult situations, where despite a less than perfect view of the action, they still have to call the game with precision and accuracy. "We've had a few bad locations more recently," Gino reflected, "After the last ownership change in Washington, the new owner (Daniel Snyder) took press box seats away for luxury seating. He moved the radio booth from its midfield location, so now we're actually behind the end line of the end zone and are down very low."

"That's the worst broadcast location I've ever had, including at high school games." Gil agreed. "It's awful. They put the visiting radio very low in the bloody end zone. It's very difficult to tell yard lines, where the ball is, and who the hell has it. I realize the fans that buy seats and have that view can't really see what's going on. But they're not being paid to tell people what's going on at the other end. They're paying to be there, to watch. I'm being paid to tell people who are not there what's going on. They put us in a position where we can't really see it. It's a disgrace.

Every NFL announcer who has to go into Washington says the same thing. After many complaints the NFL went to the Redskins and asked, 'Can't you do anything about this?' And they said no. That's why everybody likes to see (Redskins owner) Daniel Snyder lose. I've been down at the five-yard line in other places. That's not a terrific view, but if you're high enough, you can call the game. It's not that bad, but that place (Washington) is a disaster."

Gil continued to discuss less than perfect sightlines at various stadiums and talked of one lesson he learned. "I remember calling an extra point good and it was no good. But from our angle, it looked good. That happened early in my Patriots days and I learned from that not to look at the football. Look at the official under the goalposts. Fans in the end zone with the kick coming toward them will react faster. They can see whether it's going to be good. I've got to wait for the referee. When he signals it, that's when I say the kick is good. I learned the hard way."

Sometimes getting there was half the fun for Gil and Gino as they have traversed the country together countless times. Some of the road trips were more memorable than others. "We were doing both Boston College and Patriots games together from 1972 to 1976. We did a BC game at home on a Saturday afternoon and on Sunday the Patriots were playing in San Diego. We had to make a mad dash for the airport and Gino's driving like nobody's business. I mean he's really going! We were going on American Airlines and they had a check-in at the gate. We'd go to this one central area to check in. Gino said, 'How are we going to do this?' I said, 'You drop me off in front. I'll take the bags. I'll run down and check us both in. You come down and we'll hop on the plane and go.'

" I go in and head to the desk to check us in and there's an old man, an old woman, and two little kids talking to a guy from the airline. He's a guy who worked at Logan with a suit and tie on and he's saying to them loudly with his arms out, 'You want fly Nicaragua!' And the man is saying, 'No, no, no, no!' I don't pay any attention to him. I go to the desk and get our seat assignments. I turn around and I'm ready to walk over to the gate and the older man taps me on the shoulder. He asks me in Portuguese whether I can speak Portuguese. And I said yes.

"So he said to me in Portuguese that the children wanted to go to the bathroom and that they wanted water. In Portuguese, agua means water. So he's saying 'agua' to this guy. And this guy is taking the only thing he understands as agua to mean Nicaragua. So he's trying to put these people on a plane to Nicaragua. And all they wanted was to get the little kids to the bathroom and have a drink of water. I laughed all the way to the West Coast on that one, saying I couldn't believe it. That's a true story."

When Gil and Gino were on the road in their early years, there was always the uncertainty of who the engineer for the broadcast would be and how well he knew his job. "We used to hire engineers on the road. Instead of the station sending an engineer, you hired a guy locally at whatever city you were in," chuckled Gil. "We're in New Orleans at the old Sugar Bowl. It's a night exhibition game and a thunder-and-lightning storm starts. It's off in the distance, but it's raining like crazy. We take a commercial break and Gino says, 'Hey, that lightning is not that far away!'

"I said we're okay. He said, 'We're okay? That's a corrugated metal roof above us!' And it was. You could hear the rain whipping on it. He says, 'Suppose the lightning hits that!' to which I said, 'Just don't touch the equipment and you'll be all right. If you touch the equipment and the electricity comes through, it'll fry you right on the spot!' Of course, I'm lying. But he thought I was serious. He was sitting back from his mike with an alarmed and anxious look on his face. He was making sure he kept his hands away from everything.

"Another time, we go into the Sugar Bowl in the early 1970s. It's like an hour before the game on a Sunday afternoon and the engineer's not there yet. So I called the station and told them about it. They said they'd call the company that sends guys out to us all over the country. So they called me back in a couple of minutes and said they assigned a guy, but can't find him. I said to get his damn phone number. They did, called his house and his wife said, 'He's gone fishing!'

"Obviously, there was a miscommunication. So I went over to the Saints' radio station location next door. Now it's about a half-hour before the game. I said, 'Got any equipment that you can loan me?' He said no, but to call the station—I think it's WWL. So I called and said I needed an amplifier and two microphones and asked, 'Can you help me out?' The guy said he'd bring it right down.

"So now the engineer from the New Orleans broadcast comes over to my booth and says, 'You got stuff?' I said, 'Yeah, they're sending it down in a taxi.' We had the Patriots' ticket manager, Jimmy DeFrank, sitting in the booth with us. I gave him a $20 bill and said, 'Take the elevator downstairs. When the taxi pulls up with this equipment, pay for the cab and give the guy a tip. Then hustle your ass up here with the equipment.'

"The engineer from the New Orleans station comes over again and this time says 'You can't hook up that equipment, you know.' I said, "Why not?' He said, 'This is a union station. I have to hook up the equipment for you.' I asked when he could do that and he said during his first commercial break. I said, 'Oh, okay, fine' and said to myself that will be the day! The game hasn't started yet. We're using phone lines for 10 minutes in pregame and here comes Jimmy with the equipment. I'd been hooking up equipment all my life for small-town radio. I know what I'm doing. So I take the equipment, put it down on the table, give it to Gino, let him talk, and tell him to take a spot break. I close the door, lock it, and start hooking up the equipment.

"Now here's the engineer from the other station and he knows what's going on. He's pounding on the door and yelling, 'Open that goddamn door! You can't do that! I'm going to file a grievance!' And I said, 'The

Family connections, celebrations, and Old-world traditions loom large in both the Santos and Cappelletti households. Here Gil enjoys a family moment with his wife Roberta and his mother Herminia on either side, daughter Kathy, son Mark, and nephew Kenneth Santos as they pose for the family photo. Photo courtesy of Gil Santos

hell with you! I've got a game to get on!' And you know what? We got on in time to do the kickoff. I ignored the guy at the door. After the game, he started giving me grief and I said, 'Look buddy, I've got a job to do. We're talking about several hundred thousand dollars worth of commercials that have to go on. Don't be a ball-buster!'"

The camaraderie that began to develop between the new broadcast team of Santos and Cappelletti during that first broadcast together from the Oakland Coliseum would get them through many similar and worse situations over the next 30-plus years. The compatibility between the

Gino speaks to a gathering honoring Gil as the New Bedford Portuguese-American Club Man-of-the-year, one of many honors and achievements Santos has earned. Likewise, Gino has been recognized by many like organizations for his talents and contributions to the community. Photo courtesy of Gil Santos

two men can be traced further back however, before the men ever teamed up professionally thanks to the extremely similar heritages they share as first-generation Americans and sons of Portuguese and Italian immigrants. "Traditions, particularly Roman Catholic feast days, are very important in both nationalities," Santos points out. "The parishes had these big lavish feasts that ran two to three days over a weekend. Both of us grew up speaking our parents' language at home and we had a great appreciation for food."

Santos' reference to similar backgrounds was putting it mildly. "Portuguese and Italians love to eat. A meal is not a meal—it's an event. Every meal is like that, a feast. There are the meals, the work ethic, and the 'you have to get an education' ethic. There's a great love of family with a warm, passionate kind of people. And Gino and I celebrate our love of food on road trips, going out to a big dinner on Saturday nights before a Sunday game. Everything's a feast."

This has been going on for years. For Gil, it has been 32 out of the last 43 Patriots seasons. For Gino it has been 28 years. As a dining duo, Gil and Gino have been sampling gastronomical delights in every NFL city around the country for 24 years together before each game (a list of some of Gil and Gino's top picks is included as an appendix to this book).

Gino also remembered a couple of rather unusual nights out for dinner from his playing days, "There were 12 of us in Houston. We get in late and we're going to have dinner in the hotel dining room. We got the hors d'oeuvres and two hours later, the kitchen help went on

Gil and Gino resumed their Patriots broadcasting partnership in 1991 and will be celebrating a total of 25 years as the Pats Radio team during the 2008 season. Photo courtesy of Gino Cappelletti

strike!...Another time, we were in Denver. Tom Yewcic, then the special teams coach, and I like Chinese food. We asked the guy at the hotel and he suggested a real good Chinese restaurant about a half-hour away. But when we got there, the Chinese cook had quit that day. The only thing we could have was steak."

The dining-out story that tops them all has to be the one where Gil and Gino met up with the outrageously funny and unpredictable Tom Doyle in Atlanta. Tom, a 31-year broadcasting veteran, has been a radio personality on Boston radio since 1978. "I first met Gino when WHDH had the Patriots in 1985," recalled Doyle. "I had been working with WCOZ which was affiliated with 'HDH...I had been working with them for three years from 1978 to 1981. Then I was gone. I went to the West Coast and Florida. When I came back in 1985 I met Gino and we hit it off right away. Ever since he's been like family to me."

Tom Doyle is currently on Boston's WROR-FM (105.7) morning team with long time favorites Loren Owens and Wally Brine and is famous for his hilarious voice characters and comic relief in the form of his musical parodies. For the uninitiated, a few examples of Tom's rare sense of humor might prove enlightening. One of Tom's most renowned and hilarious song parodies is called "The Rectum of Edmund Fitzgerald," about a man's colonoscopy experience, sung to the tune of "The Wreck of the Edmund Fitzgerald" made famous by Gordon Lightfoot. Another great example might be Tom's "Fifty Ways to Kill a Plover," about the endangered Massachusetts seabird, to the tune of Paul Simon's "Fifty Ways to Leave Your Lover." That's Tom. That's his humor.

Tom's enduring friendship with Gino naturally became a friendship with Gil Santos for almost as long. It was no surprise to either of them that Tom showed up in Atlanta when the Patriots were down there for a game in 1992. As usual Gil, Gino, and friends were taking in a great dinner and a night out on the town before the game. This night, it included Tom.

"We had dinner the night before the game at Bone's Restaurant in Atlanta," recalled Gino. "It's one of the best steak houses in America. The manager used to work for me at The Point After in Boston. He moved down to Atlanta some years after and stayed in the business and became the general manager of Bone's, which is very popular with the sports crowd. So, we go down there and have dinner and a few drinks. Now afterward we get in a cab and there are five of us.

"Gil and two others are in back and Tom and I are in front. I'm on the outside riding shotgun and Tom is in the middle practically sitting on the leg of the driver with his arms around both of us—the very uncomfortable looking cabby and me. We were heading over to a club called The Brave Falcon. Now everybody's had a few drinks, a good meal, and was feeling good but it was very quiet in the cab for a moment before we took off. All of a sudden Tom broke the awkward silence in his own inimitable way. Mimicking Richard Simmons, he very theatrically said, 'Say fellows, I've got a *great* idea! Let's sing some show tunes!'

"Well, the cab driver practically pushed himself right through his window to get away from Tom, and Gil almost fell out of the door in the back because he was laughing so hard! To this day we haven't gotten over it! Every once in a while when we get in a cab, in any city in the country, and if it gets a little quiet, Gil will say, 'I've got a great idea, let's sing some show tunes!'"

Gil and Gino's great adventure with Tom Doyle was not over that night. It continued in a most amusing way at the game the next day. "When we were out to dinner, Tom kept asking if I can get him in the booth for the game. So I got him a pass for him to come in our booth to watch the game. Well, Tom shows up as the game was underway and comes in our rather ordinary booth and stands where all the equipment was. There was another booth next to ours, separated by a glass wall. It was empty and they had some trays of food and drinks all set up. It wasn't a really lavish booth like you see in some places, but it was pretty nice. It turns out it was the owner's booth—not the one he used personally, but one he had for some of his VIP friends to use as his guest.

"As Tom watched us work, he kept looking over at this empty relatively luxurious booth next to us and nobody was going in there—it remained empty. So before you know it, I turned around to see how he was doing. He was gone! I said, 'Where's Tom?' I looked over to the booth next door and he's sprawled out in a big stuffed chair and he's got the whole booth to himself eating and drinking and waving to us. I said, 'I'll be darned!' Tom then proceeded to have a few of his friends who were at the game join him in the box. Soon there were several friends of Tom's eating and drinking courtesy of the Falcons."

"I'm with three or four buddies of mine," confirmed Doyle, "The Patriots are winning. We are having a grand old time. All of a sudden this security guard or someone in a peach-colored sports jacket comes in and says, 'What the *hell* are y'all doing in here?' Someone in our group said, 'Ah, we were told we could sit in here.' 'Oh really?' The guy responded, 'You were told *you* could sit in here. Well, isn't this nice? You're drinking free beer, rootin' for the *wrong* team—I think you ought to get your asses out-ah he-ah!' At that point I said, 'That man right over there (pointing through the glass to Gil), see those two men over there broadcasting the game? I'm here as their guest!' So the guy leaves. The next thing I see is he's in the broadcast booth leaning over talking to Gil."

Gino remembered what happened next. "Now, Gil is live on the air talking and we hear a bunch of noise—shouting—behind us. This security guy came in our booth demanding to know who the heck is in the owner's box over there. Gil cups the mike, turns around, and he says, 'You! Get the hell out of here! I'm working! I've got work to do, and I am broadcasting this game! I don't want to hear anything about anybody! Get out of my effin' booth!' Well, I mean Gil *really* tore into that guy. Finally, the guy turns, leaves, and goes back to throw Tom out of the booth next door. But by then Tom and his entourage were long gone."

After all the years together and after all of the adventures they have shared, Gino still recalls his immediate impression upon first meeting Gil. "It was like meeting another football player from across the country—just for that instant. You have something in common. You have a bit of an understanding of that person and he has a bit of an understanding of you because of what you go through in football. There's camaraderie, a sharing of experiences, a bonding that takes place and friendships can last a long time. That gives you some sort of relationship right away and the same thing happens for people who've gone through the same type of background growing up.

"The fact that Gil's parents were immigrants from Portugal and mine from Italy gave us something in common right there because of their work ethic, their philosophies of life, and the importance of family. And Portugal is not that far from Italy. So there's a little common bond. I think that had a little to do with our ability to have a little simpatico and understanding right away. That goes a long way when two people are working together to produce something.

"Right away, I could tell by the way he or I would say things. It might even produce a little chuckle because saying, 'I know what you mean,' provides a nice comfort zone between two people. So there's no question that may have helped us working together and even socializing because this is not one of those relationships where we work together and then go our separate ways. We have dinner every single trip we've been on. I don't think we've done anything separately. Then we come back to the hotel and share some time there, going over teams, rosters, etc. All these things developed over time, but I think going back to our roots had something to do with the bonding."

5

THE KRAFT RENAISSANCE

"Santos and Cappelletti are a great pair who will be remembered forever after calling Patriots games in their greatest era. These guys are great and they belong with the great Boston sports announcers like Ken Coleman and Ned Martin (Red Sox) and Fred Cusick (Bruins). Gino breaks down the game so well and makes it easy to understand. That's always a big challenge for an analyst on radio. The key is comfort and these two make the listener comfortable following a game."—**DON ORSILLO**, NEW ENGLAND SPORTS NETWORK'S RED SOX PLAY-CALLER

GIL SANTOS REMEMBERED how New England was New York Giants country prior to 1960—that was the closest professional football team to Boston before the Patriots were established. It wasn't an easy transition for the older fans who grew up rooting for New York, but the Patriots had an opportunity to attract a whole new generation of fans—the Baby Boomers. "The development of the Patriots fan base starts with the team having to win over the fans who watched the Giants—because that was the team you saw on television every weekend around here. But the young fan, the 12-year-old kid in 1960, didn't have an allegiance so that's where a lot of the fans you see today began their allegiance to the Pats."

On Patriots founder and first owner Billy Sullivan, Santos added, "A lot of people maligned Billy Sullivan, but without him there would be no Patriots. Credit Sullivan with starting it and keeping it going. It was a budgetary tight fit. They played at Boston University, Harvard, Boston College, and Fenway Park. Then when Schaefer Stadium finally was built 11 years after the franchise was born, we thought it was phenomenal. We had our own stadium, but same people who knocked Sullivan knocked the new stadium as well, saying it was difficult to get to."

Gino Cappelletti remembers well the Patriots' shaky beginning. As one of the original Patriots he recalls the scheme Billy Sullivan put together to purchase the franchise for the new league's buy-in price of a quarter of a million dollars. Billy Sullivan did not have that kind of money, but he did have a plan. "Billy gathered nine other businessmen who put up $25,000 each," Gino recalls. "They included Dom DiMaggio." Gino mentioned that some of the others included Dean Boylan from Boston Sand and Gravel, George Sargent brother of the former Massachusetts governor Francis W. Sargent, Colonel Dan Marr of Marr Construction, and Ed Turner from Seven-Up as several investors who helped Sullivan pull the deal off. Because Sullivan was the one to bring in the rest, he held the position of president of the organization and became the public face of the Patriots management.

"Detractors knew Sullivan and his group along with the owners of the other original seven AFL franchises as the 'Foolish Club.' But as time would prove, that tag became a badge of honor as the AFL found success," said Cappelletti.

Later on, when the Sullivan family saw an opportunity to assume sole control of the team, Billy Sullivan came up with another plan to finance that venture. They made the Boston Patriots a public company and sold stock in the franchise. Many investors, large and small, bought into the team. Sullivan then made a take-over bid and bought the team from the stockholders at an undervalued price per share, according to many investors. The rancor in terms of legal action that stockholders brought against Sullivan years later haunted Billy and the franchise until the matter was settled in court and until Sullivan sold the team in 1988 to Victor Kiam, the CEO of Connecticut-based Remington Products, Incorporated. Kiam then sold controlling rights to the franchise in 1991 to St. Louis businessman James B. Orthwein who held the reins for just a brief period with the intention of possibly moving the team to St. Louis. In 1994 present owner Robert Kraft bought the team and has turned it into the most successful and well-run franchise in the NFL. He also built the state-of-the-art stadium in Foxboro to replace the decrepit and cheaply built 1970s arena the Pats called home for three decades.

The early Patriots were never truly at home during their first ten years in Boston. Their so-called home fields changed often, resulting in games at two different Boston sites in the same season on occasion due to scheduling conflicts. They even played "home" games at San Diego Stadium in 1967 (the Red Sox were in the World Series and had first priority at Fenway Park) and at Legion Field in Birmingham in 1968 for a promotional game against the New York Jets with Alabama born quarterback Joe Namath. "The first home field, for the first two years in 1960 and 1961, was the old Braves Field, or Nickerson Field as it was also

called at Boston University," Gino said. "Then we went to Boston College in Alumni Stadium for 1962. Then we moved to Fenway Park for
1963–68 and then we went back to BC for a year, then to Harvard for
another year in 1970."

So those early Patriots had four homes, none of them their own, until
the NFL-AFL merger happened and all the franchises needed to meet
certain NFL minimum home-field standards. "That meant we needed
to have a big improvement. So Schaefer Stadium was built (in Foxboro,
Massachusetts) and we began playing there in 1971," Cappelletti said.
The building of the first Patriots stadium in Foxboro (officially spelled
Foxborough, but more commonly spelled without the -ugh) is a story in
itself. After playing in four rented venues and with pressure from the
National Football League as the anticipated AFL-NFL merger became
a reality, a new Patriots stadium was clearly required. For the franchise
to survive in the region, an acceptable permanent home had to be secured.

Proposals for a stadium on the Boston Waterfront, in southern New
Hampshire, or numerous other locations in and around Boston were
lead stories on the sports pages of the region's newspapers for years prior
to the realization of a facility on US Route One in Foxboro, halfway between Boston and Providence.

Boston Herald columnist Joe Fitzgerald remembers reports of Billy
Sullivan considering a Patriots move before the development of the stadium in Foxboro. "Sullivan sought a publicly financed stadium. He
wanted one with a retractable dome in the Neponset section of Dorch-
ester but wound up going to Foxboro instead and without public fund-
ing."

Fitzgerald noted that at the time, "Sullivan could have succumbed to
overtures from cities like Birmingham and Memphis, who wanted the
Pats, so people around here should be ever-grateful to Billy for keeping
the franchise here. Billy Sullivan should be remembered for that and not
for the disarray among the investors."

Foxboro Stadium came about when the owners of the Bay State Race-
way (harness racing track) in Foxboro offered a land deal that made possible the construction of a 60,000-seat concrete football bowl—for the
bargain basement price of somewhere between $6 and $7 million.
Ground was broken in the spring of 1970 after the citizens of the then
tiny town of Foxboro voted 1,852-84 on April 13, 1970 in favor of a special zoning regulation that cleared the way for the construction.

The crucial vote was taken at the same time the headlines of the *Boston Herald Traveler* announced that the third Apollo moon-landing mission was called off as a result of Apollo 13's loss of power putting the lives of the three astronauts on board in peril. Thankfully, the Apollo 13 astronauts made it safely back to earth, and the stadium that would be known as Schaefer Stadium was complete in time for the first home game of the 1971 season.

Before the Robert Kraft ownership era began in 1994—an era that has transformed the Patriots from struggling status to reaching four Super Bowls in seven years (and five in the past 11 years)—there was a colorful sequence of coaches. It started with the franchise's birth in 1960, when team owner Billy Sullivan hired Lou Saban as the first coach when gas was 31 cents a gallon, and a postage stamp cost four cents. Lamar Hunt, an oil billionaire, couldn't get an NFL franchise, so he started his own league—the American Football League. And with a lot of help from investors, Billy Sullivan received the Boston franchise. With a flair for public relations, Sullivan held a contest to name the team and winning name was, of course, the Patriots.

Gino said Saban (with a record of 7–12–0) was fired halfway through his second season after Sullivan heard grumbling and complaints from some players, Saban having worked them through long practice sessions. Gino said. "Lou was fair to me and encouraged me, and I was happy just to be on the team." Saban went on to achieve success winning two championships with Buffalo.

In 1961 Mike Holovak replaced Saban after the fifth game and was first to steer the Pats to an appearance in a championship game. "Holovak [52–46–9] did a very good job with limited playing talent," Santos recalled. "He went to the AFL championship game (losing to San Diego in 1963)." Gino added. "He led us through one adversity after another. After Mike took over, morale went sky-high. He established practice routines we could count on, stuck with schedules, and conducted practices in a very organized manner. After a 2–3 start he went 7–1–1 and just missed winning the eastern division to the Oilers."

Holovak lasted through the 1968 season, guiding the Patriots to the AFL East title in 1963 and second-place finishes four times. Gino praised his former coach for not being one to shine the spotlight on himself, something that surely is said of Cappelletti as well. Instead, both men encouraged and praised others and attracted immense popularity for doing so.

In addition to playing 11 years for the Pats and being a part of the Pats radio broadcast team for 28 seasons, Gino spent 3 more years on the Patriots sidelines (1979–1981) as the Patriots special teams coach on Ron Erhardt's staff. Photo courtesy of Gino Cappelletti

"When I count my blessings, I think of what Mike has meant to me and my career," Gino said about Holovak. "What a coach and what a guy to play for! He loved everything about the game of football. He wore many hats— coach, travel secretary, and general manager. And loyalty was extremely important to him. It was difficult for him to let players go." Gino also recalled with a smile that he also never, ever, was heard to cuss or swear. "That was a very unusual but admirable trait for a football coach. Wouldn't you say? Personally, he taught me how to believe in myself. He had more faith in my abilities than I had in myself at the time. He helped make me more confident and thus a better player."

Cappelletti has known every head coach of the Patriots since the team's inception in 1960, either as a player, fellow coach, observer, or announcer for the team and has observed the general philosophy that governed the coaches and the game. "There are so many changes to the game because of what has evolved. The speed of the game has altered a lot of the strategies. For example the pass coverage was mainly man to man, where today they are variations of zones. Clock management and sideline management is much more demanding today. Game plans can change early on and adjustments can be made much earlier in the game than halftime. Plus the overall team concept of everybody knowing what the play is designed for and how it is executed is more pronounced today."

"In 1971, quarterback Jim Plunkett (the Heisman Trophy winning quarterback out of Stanford) was very important," observed Gil Santos of the past Patriots. "He gave the team credibility in its first NFL year

but the team had two more really awful years with John Mazur [9–21–0] as head coach.

Desperate for a nationally known coach with a reputation for winning and with the credibility to straighten out the mess in Foxboro, the Patriots offered Joe Paterno of Penn State a million dollars to come to New England. It was a lot of money. Joe was reportedly making about $30,000 a year at Penn State at a time when the starting salary for a Boston public school teacher was around $6,000. Paterno accepted the Pats job, but suddenly changed his mind and withdrew from the contract.

Gino recalled, "It happened so fast. He took it one day and by the time the information got back here, he called the next morning. He said he slept on it—it was just so quick."

At the time, Gil Santos too could only react to the reports in the news regarding Paterno's decision. But after getting to know Joe during the years that Santos called the Penn State football games, he has an explanation that makes perfect sense in light of Paterno's family values and his personality. "I remember being very excited that the Patriots were about to hire him (1972) and was surprised that he accepted it and then was surprised again that he decided that he didn't want to do it. I often wondered why until I got to State College. Then I could see why. State College is a delightful college small town. It's the kind that college town you would see portrayed in the movies of the '40s, '50, or '60s. It was just a nice place to live and raise your family. And that's who he was, and is—Joe Paterno Penn State head coach. In retrospect he probably said to himself, I'm not Joe Paterno, NFL coach, I'm Joe Paterno, coach of Penn State and that is why I'm staying."

So instead of Joe Paterno it was Chuck Fairbanks who became the new head coach of the Patriots. Fairbanks came along and got them to be a pretty good team in the mid 1970s with Steve Grogan at the helm. However the most bizarre moment in Patriots coaching history also came at the end of the 1973–78 Chuck Fairbanks era.

Santos recalled that Fairbanks [46–39–0] "had a great ability to pick players and assistant coaches and delegate authority. That was the remarkable thing about Fairbanks. He was very calm—like Belichick and unlike Bill Parcells [32–32–0], who was so bombastic. Fairbanks was more even-tempered over a game, like Belichick, and successful too—more so than coaches crashing up and down." Former Patriots general manager Pat Sullivan, Billy's son, has a fond memory of Fairbanks, though his dad—suspicious that Fairbanks was about to break his contract—removed him after the Pats won their first outright divisional title in 1978 and before the season was finished. Billy replaced Fairbanks with co-head coaches Ron Erhardt and Hank Bullough and the AFC East champions lost the season finale at Miami (23–3) and their AFC playoff to Houston (31–14). Fairbanks did go on to coach at the University of Colorado the next season as suspected and Erhardt [21–27–0] became the sole head Patriots coach from 1979 to 1981.

"The players had faith in Chuck Fairbanks," remembers Pat Sullivan. "I thought he coached our best teams in 1976 [when the Pats lost the AFC wild-card playoff to eventual Super Bowl champion Oakland, 24–21, in the final 10 seconds] and 1978." Both teams amassed 11–5 records.

The Sullivans themselves had their share of strange incidents, especially with the Oakland Raiders in Oakland. "There were two things about playing in Oakland—very long grass and a wet field," Pat Sullivan remembers. "That was a typical Al Davis move. You might as well have been in a swamp in Louisiana. Al needed to slow us down. We were young and they were old." What Sullivan was referring to was the often-suspected tactic of Davis to soak the field with water to make it soggy in order to slow down visiting teams. Of course only certain parts were soaked, others were left dry and the locations were only known to the home team so that they could operate with impunity—running plays in the dry parts and luring the opposition to the wet parts when needed.

Another strange happening in Oakland was Pat Sullivan's postgame battle with Mat Millen. Joe Fitzgerald remembered the Millen-Sullivan incident well. "It happened January 5, 1986 in the LA Coliseum just after the Patriots had finished knocking off the LA Raiders, 27–20 in the postseason. They were a wild-card entry and beat the Jets, Raiders, and Dolphins on the road en route to the Super Bowl in New Orleans that they lost to the Chicago Bears.

"Pat Sullivan, who some said had no business being on the field, was yelling at both Howie Long and Millen, a linebacker. The incident happened just after the game ended [in an end zone]. Sullivan had been barking at both players during the game, but Millen took exception just after the finish, undoubtedly upset that his team had lost to New England for a change. Millen was incensed over the 'bush play' charges that Sullivan had yelled."

Sullivan later regretted being involved in a confrontation and taking focus from a great Patriots victory. "I said not a word to Millen," insisted

Sullivan. "Howie Long was the guy. How could I be so dumb and do it in such a way to take credit away from the team, particularly the offensive line that dominated Oakland so well in that game? We beat the Raiders—the most successful game I remember from our era."

Pat looked back with fondness over his father's thinking when he started the Patriots franchise. "My dad said, 'I know this market [Boston] will be great and it will accept football.' He made it a pre-condition that the team would have to stay in Boston. 'New England is our oyster,' he always said to me."

Santos has a distinct recollection of some of the other Patriot coaches before Kraft's 1994 purchase. "Raymond Berry [48–39–0] was a players' coach—very nice. He was the right one at the right time. He took the Patriots to the [1986] Super Bowl, where they lost to Chicago. Berry replaced Ron Meyer [18–15–0], who was a disaster in terms of players following him. Berry was perfect after the turmoil of Meyer. He was a great NFL player with the Baltimore Colts who took the team to the Super Bowl with a calming personality. Unfortunately, after the Super Bowl, it came out that the team had numerous players involved with drugs—cocaine in particular—and the franchise had to begin anew to right itself."

Berry lasted until 1990 and was replaced by Rod Rust. Rust didn't last long. He was sacked after just one dismal season, the worst ever in the 30-year history of the team—a disastrous 1–15 record. The likeable and grandfatherly Dick MacPherson from Syracuse University took over to stem the tide for a couple of years but still only managed eight wins and suffered 24 losses. Finally things began to improve in 1993 with the arrival of Bill Parcells. After leading the New York Giants to two Super Bowls in 1986 and 1990, his hiring by the Patriots brought some desperately needed credibility to Foxboro.

Meanwhile, Schaefer Stadium had been renamed Sullivan Stadium after the Pats' original owner in 1983. It became Foxboro Stadium in 1990 and remained the team's home after K-Korp, owned by Robert Kraft and partner Steve Karp, bought the facility. Foxboro Stadium saw its last game during the 2001–2002 season playoffs and Gillette Stadium, privately financed by Kraft and his organization, opened in 2002 as the new home of the Patriots. Originally the stadium was going to be named CMGI Stadium but CMGI Investments faced financial difficulties and the deal fell through. Boston-based Gillette Corporation then picked up the naming rights to the 68,000-seat facility. Santos commented, "When

Kraft bought the original stadium, that was the turning point for the franchise. Victor Kiam and James Orthwein couldn't sell the team and move it out of town. Kraft had the stadium and an iron-clad contract with the team stating that it *had* to play home games in that facility. There always were rumors that the team would move somewhere (e.g., St. Louis). But Kraft owned the lease, would not let it go, and Kraft was in an ideal position to get control of the team. The greatest day in Patriots' history was when he got the team and stadium. Now they're a model franchise. Kraft runs it like his other businesses. He puts quality people (such as son Jonathan) in areas of great responsibility. He's had a perfect marriage with head coach Bill Belichick, and Robert Kraft is a straight shooter."

As a first-hand observer of the evolution of the Patriots—from a team that went from two wins and 14 losses in the 1992 season to perennial contenders and multiple Super Bowl Champions under the guidance of Kraft, his family, and his corporation—Gino Cappelletti remarked, "I'm so amazed and thrilled at what's happened since Robert Kraft bought the team and took it over in 1994. He made a very strategic move in acquiring the team by buying the stadium first. That meant the team couldn't go anywhere because he had a lease until 2002. There'd been talk when previous team owner James Orthwein came in and spoke about moving the team to St. Louis. But they couldn't have moved. Kraft had a lease here until 2002. Kraft had bought Steve Karp's interest in the stadium."

Cappelletti continued his thoughts on the subject. "Kraft did everything right and wound up with the team. And to sell out the very first year was amazing. I believe he sold 50,000 season tickets and had the other 10–12,000 for game-day sales.

"Orthwein had coach Bill Parcells as a commodity to help sell the team. I think his approach to Kraft was probably, 'I'm selling you the team and also a major-league coach. So Kraft winds up with the stadium, the team, and they're selling out the very first year of his ownership. He eventually put a good marketing team together, using his overall management skills, and putting people in position to do the job. He had Parcells and a team that started on the rise. Anyway, Kraft just brought his business acumen to his sports franchise and it worked.

"I remember [former Rams star and NBC, NFL analyst] Merlin Olsen told me once in the 1960s, 'Hey, good management will win three or four games a year.' I said, 'Hey, players win the games.' But he was right, the Kraft team proved that correct. And Kraft built the privately financed Gillette Stadium. It really is incredible what he's accomplished. In 13 years, the Patriots have won three Super Bowls in five Super Bowl appearances, won five conference championships, and eight division championships. You have to give credit where credit is due.

"I have often said that there are 32 teams in the NFL and everyone of them has ownership, executive management, coaches, and players. The difference with the Patriots, since Robert Kraft took over the team, is that the Patriots have top-notch talent—the best there is—in every one of those areas. That makes them the model franchise in the NFL, in my opinion. That is the difference and the key to their winning ways."

Kraft's control both of the team and its home venue allowed the dynamic owner to redefine what the professional football team from New England should be, and how it should operate—from security in the parking lot, to the vendors and ticket takers, to the coaching staff, and on to the players on the field.

The Kraft organization has had remarkable success in a plethora of business ventures, and Robert Kraft has been one of the most successful businessmen in America and the world. That success has been attributed by many to his sound financial planning and a business model based upon high standards, quality managers, and high expectations underscored with moral accountability.

In any of Robert Kraft's many diverse business organizations—from paper packaging, manufacturing, distribution of forest products, sports and entertainment, to equity investing and philanthropic foundations—Kraft has demonstrated a consistent philosophy, which is to put the best team of people and managers together to run each endeavor. Once in a position of responsibility, every manager is able to make critical decisions and remain relatively autonomous in doing so.

Bill Belichick is a perfect example. Belichick, through his proven abilities and demonstrated success, has the power and authority to run the football operations as he sees fit. He is of course ultimately responsible to the Kraft family for his decisions but runs the team to the best of his ability, which has proven considerable. That works within the Kraft philosophy and works with great success on the gridiron.

The Kraft organization is currently undertaking another unprecedented venture—the development of a colossal shopping and entertainment complex in Foxboro called *Patriot Place*. The project will be a "destination" complex consisting of retail stores, multiple dining and entertainment offerings, a four star hotel and spa, and even an outpatient health care center.

Besides sporting events and concerts at Gillette, a 14-screen cinema complex, a 500-seat facility for live theater, and nightclub facilities within the more upscale restaurants will offer additional entertainment options at Patriot Place. For football fans, the centerpiece of the multiple-acre development adjacent to the stadium is sure to be The Hall, the state-of-the-art Patriots Hall of Fame and Museum.

For all that he has achieved, Robert Kraft remains humble about his accomplishments and stresses that the values he holds dear in the operation of his vast business empire are solidly rooted in New England and family values—values experienced as a young boy growing up in Brookline. "When we were privileged to buy the team, it was a real challenge. The challenge was about how to run it, what to do first, and how to put all the right pieces in place. We changed a *lot* of things here. We changed the whole culture of how they did business.

"We inherited about 26 lawsuits. You *couldn't hire* a law firm in Boston because they all had a conflict of interest regarding the Patriots! It was not the way we liked to build a brand. We changed just about everything, but we did not change our radio broadcast team because they touch something in me personally. I am happy that we were able to transition *with* Gil and Gino.

"You know, you think that for 34 years before we owned the team, they never sold out one single season. The radio was actually the only way you got the Patriots because they were not often televised. So part of my memories of the Patriots was hearing them on the radio. I used to go to the games and we used to have transistor radios with us that we would listen to the call of the game on.

"Part of growing up in this area was the strong feelings about family, and community, and philanthropy—those are New England values. I knew when I bought the team that a team is a great unifier of a community. All you have to do is see how people feel on Mondays. You can see whether the team has won or lost and how that impacts the community.

"Sports also represent and are all about tradition. It's about going to a game with your kids. It's about growing up together and experiencing different great experiences. I think about that when I hear Gil and Gino's voices and you know it's the fall. It's crisp and the temperatures are getting cool. It's just a different wonderful season. I always loved the start of football season. Football was always my favorite sport and having those voices and that sense of continuity, and the tradition of listening to the Patriots on the radio, is very meaningful and very important.

"When I hear their two voices, or see them at the stadium, I feel good. I think that's true of a lot of Patriots fans wherever they are throughout New England. Gil and Gino calling the game on the radio on a New England Sunday afternoon in the fall—that's a sound that resonates well."

Robert Kraft valued the positive traditions of New England and the positive things about the Patriots football team before he became the owner of the team. Although there was much work to be done and wholesale changes in the management, operation, and almost all the personnel associated with the team, Gil Santos and Gino Cappelletti were happy exceptions for Bob Kraft. He offered the following story to illustrate his admiration for the two as broadcasters and as individuals. "When we were changing the way we did most things, we decided that there would be better coverage on radio if we went to FM. That was really revolutionary at the time! We had a lot of people mad at us because WBZ was the signal (from 1991–1995, and before that from 1966–1979) but there were lots of pockets that couldn't get the AM signal. We also wanted to have the ability to present that great parabolic stereo sound. It was very much like when I hired Belichick—I took a lot of heat for my decision. When we switched to FM, I think we were the first team in the country to do it. Now all the others have switched.

"Some of the top management on the new broadcast outlet said they wanted to make a change [in the make-up of] the broadcast team in order to appeal to a younger audience... Basically we said the team remains as it was or they were not going to get the broadcast contract. They were reluctant but they went along with it. I remember that discussion was 13 years ago and I haven't heard a peep out of them since (laughs).

"But that story says something about Gil and Gino. We changed *everything*, but we didn't change that broadcast team because in any business our family goes into, we always try and stress quality. I think that team is a *quality* championship team that we were honored to have for our broadcasts."

6

MUSINGS

"Gil Santos has one of the all-time great voices and it's natural, not like an announcer who's working hard to sound good. Gil is one of the best I've ever heard at setting up a play, which is really an important part of a radio broadcast. Gino should be in the Hall of Fame and anyone who knows him knows what a tremendous person he is. Together, they have a great rapport and you can tell, dating back to when I heard them while traveling with my dad, that they're really excited about being at the games—and were even when the Patriots weren't playing so well."
—**SEAN MCDONOUGH**, ESPN BASEBALL AND COLLEGE BASKETBALL, FORMER RED SOX TV ANNOUNCER

GIL AND GINO, more than anyone else associated with the New England Patriots, have had the opportunity to witness, report, and reflect upon the team and its owners, coaches, players, and fans. Gil has broadcasted the team for over three decades and Gino has been a player, coach, and broadcaster since the team was born they both are indelible parts of the team's history.

It is no wonder then that they have so many stories to impart and tales to tell. It seems that just when you think that they have shared them all, Gil and Gino have still more. It seems impossible to capture in a single volume all of their reflections on sports, broadcasting, and the Patriots.

"You know back in the 1970s, when they were lousy with records like 2 and 14, Gino and I had to call those games as well as the great seasons we are having now. Trust me when I tell you it's *a lot easier* to do a game when they are good because you're not trying to keep people interested in the game. People are already interested in the game because the Patriots are so good. As the announcer, all you have to do is tell them how good they are, how great this team is playing. Of course you try not to get too gushy.

"You're not going to make a bad team sound good, but trying to make a bad team's games interesting is a huge challenge—much more so than when you're with a good team and you're giving everyone happy news and 90 percent of those listening are Patriots fans. The challenge is when you have a not-so-good team and you're trying to make fans interested in the game. You're trying to make it entertaining while being honest at the same time. That's a challenge.

"I don't do the games from an angle of putting the other team down. I'm not doing them in a confrontational manner. I'm telling people where the ball is, who has it, and what they're doing with it. I'm trying to bring the whole flavor of what we're looking at, what the weather's like, where we are and how the fans are reacting. All of that comes into the call of the game. I've never had that (negative) kind of stuff happen. You can tell people what's happening without being a wise guy. You can tell them who's playing well and who isn't without being a smart ass—and without seeing if you can say something that has a double meaning—a double entendre."

Santos recalled his own broadcasting heroes and favorite sportscasters. "My all-time favorite was Mel Allen. He did the Yankee games on WINS. Even though I despised the Yankees because I was a Red Sox fan, I loved listening to Allen because he was such a great announcer. He painted a beautiful picture. He was enthusiastic and had great command of the language even though he had a bit of a Southern drawl. I thought he was just the absolute best. He could do sports, including a lot of football. He's the guy I remember most from my young childhood.

"The guy who did the Red Sox and Braves was Jim Britt and when the Braves went to Milwaukee, he went with them. Curt Gowdy came over from being Mel Allen's number two guy to take over the Red Sox. But I thought Allen was the master. You get a lot of games where I lived, down on the coast, so I listened to a lot of guys—Bob Prince (Pirates), Vin Scully (Dodgers), Red Barber (Dodgers), Harry Caray and Jack Buck doing the Cardinals. During a summer night, I'd sit there and try to find the ballgames. In the fall, I'd listen to Harry Wismer doing a big college football game every Saturday on the radio—and then Ken Coleman with some of the Cleveland Browns' games piped in here. As a teenager, I'd hear Johnny Most doing the Celtics games and Fred Cusick doing the Bruins.

"I can't remember a single radio analyst who stood out [except of course Gino today], but there was a talk show on WMGM before and after Brooklyn Dodger games. Gorgeous Gussie Moran was on with Andre Baruch and Connie Desmond. They would talk baseball—an hour show before the game and an hour after or running up to 6 o'clock.

I also was enthralled with Bob and Ray, who did a show before and after the game. And if it got rained out, they had the whole afternoon on WHDH radio.

"I met the late Mel Allen some years ago. He was in the area for an old-time radio weekend on the Cape and I had a chance to meet him. They'd re-create radio programs and bring in old stars. I was already at WBZ. I told Mel if he looked in my high school yearbook, he'd see that I put his name under 'Idol.' He was very appreciative. He was kind of a humble guy. He was very taken with that. I remember him after all these years because the Yankees, for whatever reason, dumped him unceremoniously. He was great!"

Gil has always worn two hats as a broadcaster, one as a sports reporter and the other as a play-by-play caller. But sports on the radio also includes the scores of sports talk and opinion shows—like the pre and postgame Patriots shows on WBCN hosted by moderator Gary Tanguay, with Andy Gresh, Scott Zolak, and Pete Brock. "By their very nature, sports talk shows are confrontational—whether between the hosts or with the callers. They're stating opinions. I'm stating facts," reflected Gil. "I have the 'Dog on Main Street' theory—listeners want to know about the fight. All my sportscasts are slanted locally—with the Red Sox, Bruins, Patriots, BC, UMass, etcetera. With high school basketball tourneys, I give the scores once they're into the quarterfinals. People in those towns want to know how their teams made out. It's all local. I always lead with local teams and always have a local angle. Like for instance the Tampa Bay Lightning coach is from Concord-Carlisle, so I will work that into a report. That is more important to New England fans. I don't like to listen to sports arguments. Very often, those expressing opinions don't know the whole story. I hung up on an out-of-town guy who thought the Patriots were going to St. Louis before Kraft bought the team. They couldn't have gone anywhere because Kraft had the lease. I said, 'Don't call here again.' I still don't talk to anyone from that station, even though he's been gone for years. I have opinions based on fact."

Before Tom Brady began a habit of engineering Super Bowl triumphs, Gil Santos did not hesitate to say that Celtics legend Larry Bird was the best player he ever covered in his long radio-TV career. But now he amends that: "Bird is the best basketball player, but Brady is the best I've covered in football," he declares with diplomacy. "And I would not want to say who's first and second over-all!"

Brady started his string of Super Bowl successes with that February 3, 2002 upset of the St. Louis Rams when he directed and passed the Pats downfield, setting up Adam Vinatieri for the winning 48-yard field goal as time expired.

The Brady-Vinatieri combination was obviously a huge part of the Pats' offensive arsenal and contributed mightily to both the sure thing scoring ability of the team, to say nothing of the psychological advantage it gave to the Patriots when they were just about anywhere in the opposition's territory. Why then didn't the Patriots protect record-setting place-kicker Vinatieri and instead let him become a free agent, and sign with the archrival Colts? Cappelletti offered: "The Patriots thought he'd come back to them." Indeed, they seemed shocked that their star kicker since 1986 had bolted to Indy. The golden kicker who broke Cappelletti's long held team scoring record (1,130) with 1,158 points, who won two Super Bowls with dramatic game-ending field goals and who provided the three-point margin in a Super Bowl win over Philadelphia, was gone!

Santos said he did not know Belichick's exact thinking on leaving Vinatieri unprotected and able to depart, but offered a theory about how Belichick allows players to exit before their skills decline. "I've read about how he deals with players whose contracts are up. He's not afraid to get rid of a player a year too soon rather than a year too late.

"When they won the Super Bowl after the 2001 season, he did it with a whole bunch of unrestricted free agents that he had signed, and so on and so forth. That's how he built this team—the Red Sox have followed the Patriots' path. Not the other way around. This was Belichick's way from day one. And one general manager said after that game...and I don't know exactly who said it now, but what I remember is someone said, 'That was the greatest coaching job in the history of the National Football League—he just won the Super Bowl with a waiver wire team!' Well, it really wasn't a waiver wire team but it was a team that Bill handpicked. He puts his teams together by saying I want this kind of an attitude, I want this type of intelligence, I want selfless players, I don't want ego problems. It's, you know, one for all and all for one. We win together—we lose together. I don't want any bullshit about Joe Bananas being a star.

"They would rather get rid of a player a year too soon than a year too late. Others have said this about the Patriots—they are uncanny at making personnel changes at the right time. And they are not afraid to let a player go a year too soon, rather than keep him and let him go a year too late. Very few, if any, of the players who've left, have gone on to great success somewhere else." Santos rattled off such names as Willie McGinest, Ted Washington, Lawyer Milloy, and Deion Branch. He said the same thinking could be used in the trade of quarterback Drew Bledsoe to Buffalo for a 2003 first-round choice. Then he stressed how the Vinatieri and Branch situations ironically wound up putting the Pats in a better picture.

After Vinatieri signed with Indy and gave the Colts the reliable veteran place-kicker they sought, the Patriots turned to fourth-round draft choice Stephen Gostkowski—much less expensive and also deadly accurate. He booted four field goals against Houston after his 52-yarder against Chicago—the longest ever at Gillette Stadium. He was a perfect 8-for-8 in the 2006 playoffs, including a game-winning 31-yarder with 1:10 left to seal the Pats' 24–21 stunning upset at San Diego.

Branch had a protracted holdout and the Patriots wound up trading the standout wide receiver to Seattle for a 2007 first-round draft choice. But Santos quickly pointed out they dealt that draft pick to San Francisco for the 49ers' first-round 2008 draft choice and a fourth-rounder in 2007.

Santos summarized: "Branch is a very good player, but with the acquisition of Randy Moss last season, the Patriots became much, much better. [aside to Gino] How many times did we see Randy Moss play before he got to the Patriots? Three, four times maybe. We knew he was a good player, but I had no idea just how great a receiver this guy was and is. How could I have seen him play before? I always had my own game to cover. Now that I have seen him for a whole season with the Patriots I'm thinking—Holy God! It's like Bobby Orr in hockey, Bird in basketball, Ted Williams in baseball—he makes…it…look…easy!"

Whereas Gino Cappelletti says Randy Moss is the Patriots' "graceful gazelle" of a super-receiver, he finds Wes Welker is "the lunch pail type who has a spin move like I've never seen before. When a defender is bearing on top of him, Wes knows he can avoid that critical tackle. He's a gifted guy who does this as well as anyone I've seen and then he has that burst to gain big yardage."

Welker was acquired March 5, 2007 from Miami for a second-round draft pick (60th over-all) and a seventh-rounder in the 2007 draft. Welker, often the smallest player on the field at his Oklahoma City high school, wound up breaking the Patriots' single-season reception record with 112 catches. Still just 5'9" and 185 pounds, he made more catches for more yards (1,175) and more touchdowns (8) and won more games than in his two seasons *combined* with the Dolphins (2005–06). In Miami, he had made 96 catches for 1,121 yards and only one touchdown, and the Dolphins only managed a 15–17 record.

Welker snared 11 passes for a robust 122 yards and several key connections from Tom Brady in the 38–35 comeback victory over the New York Giants that capped the Patriots' perfect 16–0 regular season. Then, in the 31–20 playoff victory over pesky Jacksonville, Welker grabbed nine Brady passes for 54 yards and the third-quarter six-yard score that broke a 14–14 tie, putting the Pats ahead to stay. Another six-yard reception was a key in the drive that made it 28–17.

Cappelletti said Belichick had similar sentiments about Donte Stallworth before his brief but important stay with the Pats during the 2007 season. He became a Patriot as an unrestricted free agent on March 13, eight days after Welker came aboard. "I thought when I heard he could come here, Stallworth catches everything," Gino said. "And that's what you need. Some guys catch everything and some you're not sure about."

The veteran of five NFL seasons with the Saints and Eagles rolled up 233 receptions and 28 touchdowns, snaring 38 for 725 yards and five touchdowns for Philly in 2006. That's a glowing average of 19.1 yards per catch. Before being lost to the Pats over contractual issues, he caught three for 22 yards in the 38–35 2007 season ending win over the Giants. But his most memorable reception was the sensational over-the-shoulder catch in full stride down the right sideline during the divisional playoffs that Santos compared to Willie Mays' circus grab in the 1954 World Series. The 53-yard picture perfect catch set up Stephen Gostkowski's 35-yard field goal that put the game out of Jacksonville's reach, closing the scoring at 31–20.

While Moss, Welker, and Stallworth created an emphasis on Brady's passing game in which the Pats departed from traditional old-style grind-it-out offense, second-year running back Laurence Maroney came on in the stretch in 2007 to offer a potent rushing attack and balance.

"Maroney has a chance to be a big star," Santos lauded after he scored two late touchdowns, of six and five yards, to overtake the Giants in the regular season finale and then barreled 122 yards, scoring a big early touchdown off a heaping 22 carries in the playoff triumph over the Jaguars. He churned a tough nine yards to set up his own one-yard score and also caught two passes for 40 yards in the latter game in a tremendous effort that took the pressure off, with Moss making only one catch. Clearly, Maroney brought the Patriots their best balance of 2007–2008.

It was the first 100-yard playoff game for Maroney, the Patriots' first-round draftee from Minnesota in 2006, running 175 times for 745 yards and six touchdowns as a rookie. He gained 835 and another six scores during the Pats' historic 2007 season. The 5'11", 220-pound speedster silenced those who were critical of him before he outplayed Jacksonville's ominous tailback tandem of Maurice Jones-Drew and Fred Taylor. He had clearly grown weary of claims that he was merely a decoy for Brady's vaunted passing attack and one who ran too upright, perhaps uptight, and laterally instead of forward. "For the first half of the year, Tom and his receivers got it done," fullback Heath Evans reflected to the *Boston Globe*. "But at the most important time of the year, Laurence stepped up."

Yet despite the newfound balance and their dominating wins during the early part of the 2007 season, Santos mustered an interesting response when asked if this Patriots team was the best ever to play the game. "It's just not the same style of NFL football that was played in the 1990s or in Gino's era," the play-caller declared. "Now the Patriots throw to set up the run. It would be the greatest single-season achievement any team ever had, but comparing decades is like apples and oranges. Some 15 years ago, do you think Kyle Brady would have been a tight end? And what about the Giants' six-foot-six inch and 265-pound running back Brandon Jacobs?" Santos asked. "When Gino played, Jacobs would have been a guard or defensive tackle--and would have even been huge at either position then. Everybody's larger nowadays. That's a big part of the way this game is played now. So you really cannot compare."

One comparison that Gil and Gino did elaborate on was that of the franchise's most recent quarterbacks, naturally giving kudos to Brady but also remembering Drew Bledsoe for his often overlooked contributions that made the Patriots a perennial championship caliber club.

"Drew Bledsoe was a great kid with a great arm. Whatever it is that Brady has—Drew did not. Whatever that indefinable something is, and that's not a knock on Drew, it's just that Brady has an indefinable something that quite frankly I haven't seen any other Patriot quarterback have, with the possible exception of Grogan," explained Gil. "Drew obviously had a great arm. He lacked mobility. And I don't know if he saw the field as well as some quarterbacks do. I don't know if that is a gift or an acquired talent or what. Drew's critics should know that once he got to the Patriots, they did not have a game that was not a sell-out—regular season, exhibition, or postseason.

"Parcells drafted Bledsoe and gave the Patriots a certain cachet and credibility. I remember Bledsoe being a great college quarterback with a big strong arm that could throw the ball through a wall, and his ability to bring the team from behind in a game. I remember one vividly—the game against the Vikings at Foxboro. They were behind 24–0. He brought them back to win in overtime. So, in the early years that Bledsoe had, he did so many things to help create the franchise that the Patriots now have become. I don't think people have given him credit for that. People obviously remember to credit Kraft for the changes in Foxboro, they remember Parcells, and there are a lot of people who were critical of Bledsoe and in their adoration for Brady overlook the contributions that Bledsoe made. I mean, hey, he came here in 1993, we were in the Super Bowl in 1996 (actually played in January 1997, vs. Green Bay). That didn't happen by accident.

"I'm sure that he would have enjoyed being involved more than he was in the first Super Bowl victory in 2002 but he showed a lot of class in being supportive of Brady and what the team was doing at that time because it was on the upward and onward road then. I remember when Brady got hurt in that Pittsburgh game. I remember saying on the air how tough it was to lose Brady in this game, but how many teams can have a Drew Bledsoe come off the bench to replace him in a championship game—a guy of his ability. And he got us down into the end zone pretty quick!"

When asked to assess Tom Brady's All-Pro talent, Gil Santos puts his answer in one all-encompassing sentence: "He was born to lead." He elaborated before the January 2008 American Football Conference title game against San Diego in Foxboro: "Paraphrasing the words of Herb Brooks, who told the U.S. hockey team before upsetting the Russians in the Olympics: You were born to be here at this time and to go out and win at this game! I find that's a great way to put it regarding Brady. Brady was born to do this—he leads by doing. He's the Comeback Kid, too. I think there have been 27 or 28 times now that he's brought the Patriots back from behind or a tie in the fourth quarter to win."

Gino Cappelletti explained Brady's mystique further: "He thrives on competition and coming from behind to win. He looks for it. To him, it's the challenge of all challenges. One of the most exciting things in sport is for a fighter to come off the canvas and find a way to win. That's Brady. Brady's teammates feel it too and they respond!"

After firing an NFL record 50 touchdown passes in the 2007 regular season, breaking the standard set by Indianapolis' Peyton Manning, he lofted three more touchdown receptions in completing 26 of 28 passes for a league-mark 92 percent playoff completion rate in the opening-round victory over Jacksonville. During the season, 23 of his completions went to top receiver Randy Moss—another NFL mark. And he directed the Pats with that amazing accuracy to a league-record 589 points, eclipsing the mark of 556 by the 1998 Minnesota Vikings. Not bad for a sixth-round draft choice.

Ever since displacing Drew Bledsoe as the Patriots quarterback, he has led the Pats to greatness—especially their three Super Bowl triumphs over highly favored St. Louis, then Carolina, and Philadelphia. He's the only quarterback in NFL history to start and win three Super Bowls before his 28th birthday.

Cappelletti had an ideal comparison for Brady. "He's like a duck in water—calm and collected on top but underneath he's paddling like hell. He has the fire in his belly. You can see it in his eyes when he's on the sideline. On the playing field, he's cool, calm, and collected. This is what the players respond to—he ignites the whole team." Cappelletti also calls Brady "the master technician you'd want at quarterback. He's made Bill Belichick a better coach and Belichick made Brady a better quarterback.

"Tom Brady displays a quarterback talent we haven't seen for awhile. You just see it every so often—from Johnny Unitas, Joe Montana, John Elway—that type of quarterback. He has such a record now. It shows he makes very, very few mistakes. He has quick reads. The ball comes out so fast. That's part of the system the Patriots have employed and his ability to fit that system makes him tops. That's the reason they got rid of [Drew] Bledsoe. Brady's quarterbacking was more adaptable to the system they're employing. Bledsoe's style was to get back, wait till the receiver got open, and gun it in there. He had that kind of strong arm whereas Brady can anticipate a little bit. The ball comes out and the receiver and ball meet. He's so cool and he's cool in the huddle, just stays calm even with time running out. He wins overtime games and so you can play for overtime. That's good for the team because there's a history of knowing how to win and what it takes to win in overtime."

Gino continued, "Brady has that ability to lead on the field as a coach would like their quarterbacks to do. He's like one of the coaches and he's executing the plays. He's obviously very bright and handles himself well. He has a great demeanor on the field. You can see he has the passion, that he's not the kind of guy who's going to berate anybody. But he may pump up somebody in his own manner. Some quarterbacks really get on a player out on the field. He's not that type. He does it with his execution—by example."

Santos calls Brady "the calmest quarterback under pressure that I've ever seen. You can see his insatiable desire to win. He has that sixth sense. If someone is coming up from behind him, he senses it. He's so cool, so smart. And as soon as the ball is snapped, he knows where to go with it. Another thing—the game is so slow for Brady. He can see the action as if it was in slow motion. The game slows down for the great players. If there were three seconds left in a game, Larry Bird would get the winning shot off in two and a half seconds. Tom Brady has that same ability."

Santos could not help but to again compare the talents of Larry Bird and Tom Brady. "They're very similar in not panicking at crunch time," he declared. "Both are very confident. Bird said nonchalantly after winning a game by three points, 'It was all right. The ball was in my hands and I knew we're gonna win.' I remember one game in Milwaukee, he put up a shot from the corner and without even watching it, he walked off the court as the ball went swish at the finish."

Tom Brady is that same way at crunch time. Brady started his string of Super Bowl successes with that February 3, 2002 last-second upset of the St. Louis Rams—"I wasn't surprised at all," Santos said. "The Patriots had 1:17 left when they got the ball. That's a lot of time. And I knew Vinatieri would make that kick." He did, and the Patriots had the first Super Bowl victory in their 42-year history, 20–17—because Brady and Vinatieri, like Bird, shared one thing: they were cool at crunch time.

Part Two

A TALE OF
TWO SEASONS

7

THE EARLY GAMES

"Santos and Cappelletti are great—and part of the fabric of New England. Gil has been waking us up for decades with sports on WBZ and Gino is a perfect complement to him on Patriots' broadcasts. The best thing is that Gil grew up here and has that encyclopedia mind, meaning he doesn't have to look up what happened in the past because he lived it. And Gino, who belongs in the Hall of Fame, played and coached with the Patriots dating to their start, so he lived it too."
—**MIKE LYNCH**, WCVB TV SPORTS ANCHOR, AND TV HOST OF *PATRIOTS FIFTH QUARTER*

THE STORY OF THE 2007–2008 PATRIOTS seems like a tale that Charles Dickens would pen if he were a 21st century sports reporter instead of a Victorian novelist. New England football fans had such "Great Expectations" for a fairy tale ending to the incredible Patriots story as each game unfolded during the season. But when the season was all over, they instead endured a far different saga—one that might have been titled "A Tale of Two Seasons"—a fable where this time the hero did not triumph in the end.

With apologies to the late Mr. Dickens for altering the title of his famous novel, it seems most appropriate to ponder the famous opening lines from his great work, *A Tale of Two Cities*. As we look at the Patriots season of 2007–2008, his words seem so very appropriate.

> "It was the best of times, it was the worst of times... it was the epoch of belief, it was the epoch of incredulity, it was the season of Light, it was the season of Darkness, it was the spring of hope, it was the winter of despair..."

As difficult as it might be for many fans to relive the season of great expectations, 2007 just happened to be the year that the authors of this book were privileged to observe and document the legendary team of Santos and Cappelletti as they, and the WBCN Radio network crew, broadcasted one of the most exciting, emotional and amazing Patriot football seasons ever played.

The Patriots season of 2007 turned out to be one heck of an incredible season to go behind the scenes with Gil and Gino, sharing their unique and enlightening view from the booth. OK, so you know the ending, but enjoy the great stories, record-shattering performances, and amusing anecdotes that were all part of the most victorious regular season ever completed by a team in NFL history.

September 9, 2007 at New York:
New England Patriots 38, New York Jets 17

Even before the Patriots blew out the Jets at Giants Stadium in their 2007 season opener, Santos and Cappelletti sensed this New England team would be special—perhaps even more special than the three previous Super Bowl championship teams.

"We knew during that third exhibition game at Charlotte," said Santos. "That third exhibition is the one that's played like a regular season game with the starters going up to three quarters. Randy Moss didn't play in any preseason games, but the Patriots were still so dominating, we all turned to each other in the booth and thought this team has a chance to be scary.

"Then in the opener against the Jets, the Patriots followed the opening kickoff by driving 91 yards in 11 plays for a touchdown to go up 7–0." Indeed, that set the tone for the first of many Patriots routs early in the season where the Pats would score over 30 points in each victory—this time 38.

That opening game also became the infamous "Spygate" game. The suffix "gate" has been attached to any allegedly scandalous incident the media reacts to since the infamous June 1972 burglary of the Democratic National Committee headquarters at the Watergate Hotel in Washington D.C. by operatives of President Richard Nixon. Thus, there have been any number of "gates" in and out of politics since then—Travelgate, Filegate, Contragate, and Monicagate, to name a few.

When Jets coach Eric Mangini accused the Patriots of violating the NFL's rules regarding videotaping the opposing team during a game, the press quickly dubbed it "Spygate" or alternatively "Cameragate" and "Videogate." The Patriots later acknowledged that someone from the

Patriots staff was videotaping the Jets sideline from the field during the game in violation of league guidelines. The Jets argued that the Patriots were trying to intercept the Jets signals from the bench to the defensive team on the field, giving the Patriots an advantage in the game. Coming at the start of what many objective observers foresaw as a potentially great season, the "Spygate" scandal left a particularly bitter aftertaste for Patriots' fans.

Clearly, the Patriots didn't need illegal help in the form of stealing signals via a spying camera to wallop the inferior Jets, coached by former Patriots' defensive coordinator Eric Mangini. There had been bad blood between Belichick and Mangini exemplified by their cold handshake tiff the previous season. But this time, Mangini had blown the whistle on his former mentor, over what many observers felt was a minor violation and an often-common practice by most teams in the NFL. The league followed with the punishment of a huge fine and the loss of a number one draft choice.

Gil Santos lost no time in using a WBZ radio morning sports commentary to address those critics who ripped Patriots coach Bill Belichick over the "Spygate" controversy.

The media bashing of the Patriots continued long after the NFL sanction against Belichick and the team. Had the Patriots taped from the front row of the stands, rather than from the sidelines—a distance of perhaps 30 feet—there would have been no rule broken. It appears the heavy penalty was levied because the Patriots had disregarded the "letter of the law" contained within the league directive, presumably dating back to the previous season. As this season unfolded and the Patriots threatened the glory of the 1972 Miami Dolphins (1973 Super Bowl Champions) as the only unbeaten team in National Football League history (14–0 in the regular season, 17–0 including the playoffs), even former Miami Coach Don Shula added to the controversy stating that, should the Patriots go undefeated, the record books should insert an asterisk beside that record indicating that it was tainted or invalid because of the filming incident. Shula later recanted the statement and did so more than once.

Cris Collinsworth of NBC, considered by many Patriots fans to be one of the most unlikable announcers on the air, didn't win over any New England fans over when he said, "I think Commissioner Goodell blew this one. Bill Belichick should have been suspended without question. The punishment hit only their wallets and future draft choices. There is nothing that impacted this season. He should have been suspended for at least the [next] Jets game because that's where the violation occurred and, in my opinion, a playoff game. This was a great opportunity for the commissioner to lay down the law like he's done with the players, and he didn't do it."

As vehement as Collinsworth was, John Madden—who is still not a favorite of Patriots Nation after his Super Bowl gaffe in 2002—at least offered a more conciliatory thought. "I think the commissioner did a good job. Maybe it's not severe enough for Cris, but it's severe enough for the rest of the league. Commissioner Goodell sent a message not only to the Patriots but to the rest of the league." Getting back to what was taking place on the field, Madden could not help but praise the ability of the team and particularly its quarterback. "Tom Brady is playing his position better than anyone ever played it in the NFL. When you watch him play, he does what every other quarterback does, but he just makes it look that much easier."

Even as John Madden was trying to put a little perspective on the situation, Gil Santos was livid at the obsessive and irrational positions of many of the critics. "There is no doubt in my mind that some of the over-the-top and overzealous attacks on Belichick and the questioning by some of the validity of the Patriots' three Super Bowl titles has galvanized this team," Santos declared. And he was just warming up, readying a slam of his own at ex-Pats defensive coordinator Eric Mangini, now the Jets' head coach.

"They [the Pats] were already loaded with talent on both sides of the ball and special teams…they have terrific depth and now, thanks to some aspersions cast on them by media people, print and electronic, have rallied around their coach and around each other to the point they will be even tougher to beat than they were going into the season," Santos said.

He refused to criticize Belichick, the Pats, or owner Bob Kraft as many did—and the team's longtime radio play-caller knew what criticism was headed his own way. But he used a salty comparison to Mangini to answer the "homer" charge that would be leveled against him: "People will call me a homer, but I'd rather be criticized for being loyal than for being an ungrateful rat!"

September 16, 2007 at Foxboro:
New England 38, San Diego Chargers 14

The next challenge for the Patriots was a meeting with the highly-rated Western Division rival San Diego Chargers. Just seven months before, in the 2006 postseason, overwhelmingly favored San Diego was the team that the Patriots had upset for the AFC divisional crown in a West Coast shocker that still left a bitter taste on the palates of the San Diego team and their fans. After that emotional upset victory, the Pats went on to lose the AFC title game in the last moments to Indianapolis. And even in that latter game, Santos noted the Pats were just "one play away" from yet another trip to the Super Bowl.

This time around the Chargers and their vaunted offense were expected to give the Patriots a comeuppance, and it seemed that much of the national media were just waiting for the Patriots to experience their first loss of the season at the hands of such a strong West Coast team, especially after the so-called "Spygate" incident.

Prior to the game, Patriots fans tailgating outside of Gillette Stadium responded to the previous week's controversy in typical fan fashion. Signs and posters mocked the "Camera/Spygate" charges. Homemade prop video cameras created out of cardboard, plastic cups, and styrofoam were attached to the top of assorted and sundry headgear worn by scores of Patriots partisans in response to the media hype of the past week.

During the pregame introductions, the fans gave a prolonged standing ovation to coach Belichick at the mention of his name. At various times during the game, fans sitting behind or near the San Diego bench stood and derisively aimed their cameras and camera-phones towards the Chargers' bench as the national television cameras dollied past on the sidelines.

In the 8:15 p.m. nationally broadcast home opener for the Pats, without the assistance of any cameras mentioned, the Patriots shut out the Chargers with an amazing display of football prowess in the first half and went on to win convincingly 38–14. New England shut down the potent offense of the Chargers and held superstar LaDainian Tomlinson to just 43 yards on 18 carries.

Santos declared once more to his radio audience that the blowout of New York and "Spygate" had "galvanized this team even more than before. This is a very physically gifted team and questioning the three Super Bowl triumphs and our coach just was not going to happen!" And Gino declared: "The players had such respect for Bill, they went out and kicked San Diego's butt in response to all the talk about the incident."

During the game, Patriots fans had someone new, very exciting and very positive to cheer about. This powerful and talented Patriots team now had Randy Moss.

Moss had been sidelined for the entire preseason. Nobody knew how good he could be on this Patriots team until his debut in the opening game against the Jets. It turned out he was very good—very, very good! Moss had nine receptions for 183 yards and a touchdown. A 51-yard strike from Tom Brady upped his per-reception average to an impressive 20.3 yards a catch. And now against San Diego, the Moss factor proved to be no fluke but a harbinger of great things to come. It was his second 100-yard or more game in a Patriots uniform. Moss gained over 100 yards on eight receptions in the San Diego game and he scored a pair of touchdowns. It was also Moss' 50th career game of 100 yards or better.

When it was suggested that Moss had been a bad actor in the past, Santos pointed out he wasn't *that* bad. "I think his problem was immaturity and not having the right supporting cast and Tom Brady for a quarterback," Santos said. Cappelletti agreed, noting: "Now he is in the right situation with the right supporting cast, which is what he has here."

In the postseason playoffs, domestic abuse accusations against Moss surfaced to become another distraction in what was a season of distractions—some self-imposed and others created by Patriots detractors. In the case of Moss, the allegations against him would surface again in a most untimely manner during the playoffs and then news accounts shortly after the season quietly announced that his accuser had dropped the matter.

Santos pointed out something the Patriots ownership, coach, and players expected of themselves regarding the deportment and professionalism of the Patriots: "There are no bad actors here." Gino chimed in: "They're selfless." And Gil concluded: "That's Belichick."

"The record speaks for itself," Santos declared when asked to assess Belichick's importance to the Patriots' success. He's reached four Super Bowls in seven years, won three Super Bowl championships, and came close to a fourth.

"Belichick has a great eye for talent, a great eye for fitting the right pieces into the right places and a great eye for discerning another team's weaknesses and exploiting them. He's very intense and single-minded once the football season starts. He's the kind of guy who's not afraid to hire the best quality of assistant coaches. Some are afraid. He just knows football players and how they best fit the way he wants a game to be played. He's extremely smart and his players play smart. They don't make dumb mistakes," assessed Santos.

Santos thought for a moment more and reflected how Belichick had treated Gino and him. "He's always been very accommodating to us, very loyal and supportive. It's been a phenomenal run with Bill."

Cappelletti, who interviews Belichick for WBCN before every Pats game, said he respects and admires Belichick's total commitment to the game beyond coaching the team on the field—evaluation of players, business savvy in regard to that aspect of the game, scouting, the way the draft works and can impact the team, and so on. His close working relationship with Scott Pioli, the Patriots' vice-president of player personnel, is a good example of Belichick's approach to the total management of the team. "When they are looking at a player to bring in as a free agent, a draft pick, or as a trade they both have to agree," said Cappelletti. "I have heard that if Bill says yes, and Scott feels differently, or vice versa, then they both will agree that there is no deal. That is how much Belichick believes in the talent he has surrounding him and in Scott Pioli in particular.

"Before he became a head coach, Bill was a highly respected assistant coach and defensive coordinator who had great talent in breaking down an opponent's strengths and weaknesses. I think he had it ingrained in him by his father who was a great football man—playing college and professional football before being a coach at several colleges, including North Carolina, Vanderbilt, and finally Navy where he brought scouting to a fine art—and he took it to great heights.

"You've heard the saying that a team's personality reflects that of its coach. I think that's true with the Patriots." Cappelletti added, "Bill is a brilliant tactician and has shown that many games are won with 'smarts' as well as toughness. Because of that, his teams have come to enjoy the signature reputation of being cerebral as well as physical.

"Bill has a deep appreciation and respect for the traditions and integrity of the game. He is very much aware of things that are meaningful to his players and the fans, for example letting 43-year-old backup quarterback Doug Flutie dropkick the extra point in his last game, or getting 20-year veteran and backup quarterback Vinnie Testaverde into a game to throw a touchdown pass (which broke his own record of consecutive seasons with at least one TD pass)."

Gino stressed, "With Belichick, his players get a dedicated football man who tells them why they're doing certain things so they understand the concepts. He shows them and teaches them what it takes to win. Once the players bought in to his philosophy—and they did for good reason—the team became one of the elite teams in the NFL. A lot of players look forward to his information about how to attack and defend against another team. He creates many different game situations and scenarios in practice, so the players will respond instinctively and correctly if they should see a similar situation in a game. The players believe in him. As a result they perform at the highest levels and achieve remarkable things, and to me that's a characteristic of a great coach. It is my opinion that history will prove Bill Belichick to be one of the all-time great coaches."

September 23, 2007 at Foxboro:
New England Patriots 38, Buffalo Bills 7

Up next in 2007 was the Pats' third foe, Buffalo, and another rout ensued in Foxboro, 38–7. The Pats had rolled up 38 points in each of their first three games—with more and bigger blowouts to come from this incredible offense led by Brady and Moss. Buffalo had led early in the game, 7–3, but the Pats roared past like a runaway locomotive, scoring 14 points in the second period, 14 more in the third, and another seven unanswered points in the final quarter.

October 1, 2007 at Cincinnati:
New England Patriots 34, Cincinnati Bengals 13

A Monday night game in Cincinnati brought a supposedly menacing Bengal offense to the contest. But it was no contest as Brady passed the Pats to another lopsided success, 34–13, for their fourth victory. "Cincinnati came in with a high-powered offense, but the Patriots kicked their butts," Santos said.

October 7, 2007 at Foxboro:
New England Patriots 34, Cleveland Browns 17

Gino Cappelletti credits their fifth victim, the Cleveland Browns, with providing "a good physical game." But again it was another "no contest," as the Patriots were once again victorious, 34–17. Now the Patriots were beginning to really interest a national audience, as they were undefeated and were heading for a showdown with another unbeaten team, the Dallas Cowboys.

October 14, 2007 at Dallas:
New England Patriots 48, Dallas Cowboys 27

The Patriots were clearly on a roll, but so was Dallas. The Cowboys were also unbeaten, but barely so, after surviving their last outing in Buffalo on a game-ending field goal after trailing badly all night. Dallas quarterback Tony Romo tossed six interceptions in the contest to make the Cowboys' win even more difficult.

The Patriots set up the battle of unbeaten teams with an incredible offensive machine. Brady began putting his touchdown-pass express into higher acceleration with five touchdown pitches and 388 aerial yards with no interceptions, dealing Dallas its first defeat, 48–27. This performance enabled him to set a league record by realizing at least three scores in each of the season's first six games. In 2006, he threw for three scores only twice. It was clear that the arrivals of Moss, Welker, and Stallworth made his target arsenal far more effective than was the previous season's trio of Patriot receivers—Troy Brown, Reche Caldwell, and Doug Gabriel.

Stallworth, Welker, and Moss combined for 24 receptions, 319 yards, and four touchdowns as they overwhelmed the Cowboys. Brady outshined his counterpart Tony Romo—even though a Brady fumble was converted into a Dallas six-pointer. He connected with Welker twice (35 and 12 yards) and Stallworth once (for 69) on post routes. He also found Moss uncovered in the end zone for a six-yard touchdown, and Kyle Brady for a one-yard TD, as the Cowboys' secondary was no match for the Pats' receivers. Romo, meanwhile, faced a 3–4 defense for the first time in the 2007 season and threw two touchdowns in going 18-for-29 for 199 yards with one pickoff. Romo improved markedly from a six-turnover show that nearly cost defeat in Buffalo, but he still was no match for Brady.

Brady started fast, leading the Pats to a 14–0 quarter bulge as Moss and Welker caught Brady scoring tosses. But Dallas trailed by just 21–17 at halftime and actually led, 24–21, after Romo heated up with a second straight scoring pass. Then Brady got hot again, connecting with Kyle Brady and Stallworth to give New England the lead for good

(28–24) while Gostkowski added field goals of 45 and 22 yards as the Pats started to bury the Cowboys.

The audience tuned in to Santos and Cappelletti knew this game was in the bag when coach Wade Phillips (son of former Houston Oilers and New Orleans Saints head coach Bum Phillips) opted for a field goal with Dallas trailing by two touchdowns with only 10 minutes remaining. The Patriots outscored Dallas, 37–10, in the second half and answered Terrell Owens' pregame boast of an easy Dallas victory—one he predicted that would be so easy the fans could "getcha popcorn," and relax as Dallas beat New England.

Even though the Patriots fell behind in this one for a while, they rallied again to another rout, 48–27. "I had no doubt in my mind that the Patriots would come back and win going away," Santos stated.

October 21 at Miami:
New England Patriots 49, Miami Dolphins 28

The New England franchise then defeated winless Miami, 49–28, in their seventh game of the season. "They really are a machine," Cappelletti enthused in Miami, noting Brady was a perfect 11-for-11 for four scores in building a 35–7 cushion before his fifth touchdown pitch made it 42–7 at the break.

The second half was a mere formality, though Coach Bill Belichick felt he had to return Brady to the lineup for a sixth scoring strike after Matt Cassel proved ineffective. The return of Brady into the game after the brief Cassel appearance added fuel to the fire of a new line of criticism by Patriots detractors. The Pats won the first seven games of the season by scoring 34 or more points in every game, 48 or better in the last two. But critics decried that they were unfairly running up the scores. Apparently, to some people, this team was *too* good!

"Unbelievable," Santos remarked in response to the idea that anyone could find fault with a professional football team doing all it could to win the game and put points on the scoreboard—"It's what they're supposed to do!" "Unbelievable" was also Gino's sentiment, but Gino was referring to the prowess of Tom Brady and company—not the cynics.

The impressive win over Miami gave the Pats a 7–0 start for the first time in their history and Santos declared Brady "had another unworldly first half, taking no prisoners. I've never seen a Patriots first-half performance like this one." Brady had lost one running back, ex-Dolphin Sammy Morris, for the season due to injury, but saw Laurence Maroney return after missing three games with a groin injury. But the terrific Tom Brady didn't need him in moving the ball at will, connecting with Moss for two spectacular scores. The 42 first-half points set a Patriots record. Brady wound up 21-for-25 for 355 yards and the six scores. "The sky's the limit," Cappelletti raved to his audience. "The Patriots could become one of the elite teams in NFL history." Time would tell.

Gil and Gino's audience numbers into the hundreds of thousands and includes Patriots fans of all ages. Sometimes, if that young fan is *very* young, a complete understanding of what is being reported may take a little coaching from mom and dad—at least as implied in this humorous story sent into the *Boston Globe Magazine* and published in a feature called "Tales from the City" (Sunday Nov. 25, 2007). Michael Pinciaro of Beverly, Massachusetts was the contributor.

> Last month, I was driving my 3-year-old son to the park on a warm Sunday afternoon. As we listened to Gil Santos and Gino Cappelletti describe the Patriots' trouncing of the Dolphins, the [announcers] picked up the referee's call of "Timeout, Patriots."

A little voice from the back seat said, "What did the Patriots do wrong to get a timeout?"

Stay tuned, little guy, and keep listening to Gil and Gino—if you do, pretty soon you will understand anything you'll ever want to know about Patriots football.

8

INSIDE THE BOOTH

*"I have worked with both Gil and Gino on WBZ and we've all been really fortunate to have the benefit of what they do. They're real professionals with a strong passion for football. They're a remarkable combination—a great team broadcasting a great team!"—***BOB LOBEL**, LONGTIME BOSTON TELEVISION SPORTS ANCHOR

*"I don't always join Gil in the broadcast booth but I always enjoy it when I do. I used to do play-by-play for the University of Rhode Island and understand what Gil does to prepare and do the job. To see the teamwork and camaraderie amongst him, Gino, and the entire WBCN broadcast crew is a joy to watch."—***MARK KATIC**, WBZ NEWS RADIO 1030

October 28, 2007 at Foxboro:
New England Patriots 52, Washington Redskins 7

It was the halfway point in the 2007 NFL season. Expectations remained high for the 7–0 New England Patriots and their stellar lineup. Clearly, Tom Brady now had the offensive weapons every radio talk show caller had been lamenting about *not having* the previous year—superstar Randy Moss along with electric wide receivers Donte Stallworth and Wes Welker. With a healthy Laurence Maroney along with Kevin Faulk and Sammy Morris, the Pats now had a formidable proven offense— one able to win a ballgame in the air or on the ground.

Dan Dierdorf concurred with that observation on a CBS broadcast when talking about the new look of the Patriots offense, "Randy Moss changes the Patriots' entire dynamic. I've had coaches tell me that Moss is worth 50 yards a game in the running game. When Moss is on the field, you can't bring that safety up into the box. That safety has to stay over the top to double Moss. Because of that, you're only running against seven guys, not eight.... the 'Moss Effect' is helping their running game. And it's helping Donte Stallworth and Wes Welker because

Randy is getting double-coverage and these two guys are running wild all over the field."

Once again Gil Santos and Gino Cappelletti settled into the 12 by 20 foot WBCN Radio booth located on the 50-yard line directly below the exclusive Club Seat level of Gillette Stadium for the 4:15 p.m. contest. It was the late game of the nationally televised Sunday doubleheader on the Fox network, which had set up its broadcast team adjacent to The WBCN "Rock" Radio Network booth where Gil and Gino operate.

WBCN has been the flagship station for the Patriots radio network since 1995, offering the listening audience a singular experience, broadcasting in life-like stereo. Audio engineer Dennis Knudsen, a veteran of 12 seasons in the 'BCN booth, had been setting up the headsets, microphones, mixing board, and assorted other electronic gear since noontime for the afternoon broadcast. Sixteen channels on Dennis' mixer are always in play for this remote, including stereo crowd mikes (those ubiquitous clear-plastic parabolic saucers seen on the sidelines), a microphone on the head referee, a set-up in the downstairs press room for the post game interviews, a feed from the stadium public address announcer, a return channel from the WBCN studios in Boston, another feed from the WBCN broadcast tent outside of the stadium where the pre and postgame shows are broadcast from, and of course head sets and microphones for Gil, Gino, producer Marc Cappello, engineer Knudsen, and for halftime show host Gary Tanguay.

This week the Patriots were taking on the Washington Redskins of the National Football League's Eastern Conference, who even with a 4–2 record represented a threat to the perfect 7–0 New England Patriots. The Patriots had played the Redskins just seven times in their history and had only defeated the Washington team once, 35 years ago, in their first meeting in 1972. The unfamiliarity required caution and prompted meticulous preparation by the Patriots.

Meticulous preparation is also required of the Patriots radio broadcast team each week. Like the coaches and players on the field, Santos and Cappelletti, as they do throughout the season, get ready all week for game day. Working with their longtime statistician Roger Homan, who Santos often refers to on air as "*Ace* statistician Roger Homan," Gil and Gino crack the record books, study the scouting reports, conduct interviews, and talk to their sources in and out of the NFL.

Each man brings to the broadcast booth his own style and character. Santos, the play-by-play caller, has devised a unique color-coded identification chart for each player on each team, which he places on the counter before him. Washington's offensive and defensive lineups are placed on one side of the Bushnell extra-wide-angle binoculars he uses during the game, the Patriots information on the other. The placements of the lists on the counter correspond to where each team is positioned on the field. Today the Patriots will open the first quarter defending the goal to the left of the broadcasters, so Santos places the Patriots information to his left, Washington's to his right. The lists get swapped each quarter.

Gil's spotting lists are a work of art and a study in inventive, yet simple, design. He created the prototype of the homemade charts when he was covering the Penn State football team in the mid 1980s. His system is based upon the *people who handle the ball*.

Color-coded and grouped in vertical columns, all of the quarterbacks are listed in large, bold, handwritten, red letters. The running backs are grouped and listed next underneath the quarterbacks in blue, then the receivers in green, and the specialists (kickers, punters, etc.) in purple at the bottom of the first column. The defensive players form a second column on Gil's chart and are listed in black. The system holds for both teams, which means another part of Gil's homework every week is to prepare a new list for each opponent—a minimum of three hours to do the job. In addition to the names and positions, Gil has squeezed in some pertinent information about each player in a simple code he has devised so at a glance he can recite things like the number of touchdown passes a quarterback has thrown, interceptions for a defensive player, sacks for a lineman, and so on. On his home team ledger, Gil uses tiny one-inch square stickers to update his notes as often as needed. Of course, Gil is ably assisted in his play-by-play calling by statistician Homan who sits at his side and who has his own copious notes and stat books at the ready.

Gino has his own style of identifying the players and preparing for his Sunday afternoon job as commentator on anything and everything regarding the Patriots. Gino prefers to hand chart the offense and defense in a more traditional manner, one that may reflect his many years as a player and coach. "I 'play' with the offense when the Patriots have the ball, and mentally line up behind our defense when the other team is in possession," says Cappelletti about his approach to viewing and commenting on the game. "Gil and I also frequently use the term 'from left to right' or 'the Patriots are moving from right to left' so that the listener can visualize the game better. The direction we call is always in relation to the radio dial."

Roger Homan is sitting on Santos' right, in between Gil and Gino. As the statistician for the broadcast he also has his own method and improvised device—his own statistics board or chart to keep track of the game. Homan's board is a sandwich of thin Plexiglas in which a sheet of paper, printed on both sides, with blank statistical categories for each team is inserted. It is approximately 14 by 20 inches in size and the categories include the number of times the quarterback attempts a pass, how many completions, how many interceptions, and so on. Roger's board has a place for every conceivable statistic in the game. The boxes or spaces for the stats are filled in as the game goes on by marking the plastic overlay with fine point colored markers, allowing the board to be reused throughout the season. "My primary responsibility is from the kickoff to the end of the game. All the numbers that go on in that time period— that's my responsibility. I've got to give them to Gil at the most accurate and precise times. I know by listening to his broadcast over the years when he is talking about something, what he's going to want. He knows how to read my board so we can do it instantaneously."

Homan has had two tenures with Gil and Gino. His first came in 1971. "Gil and I go back to 1971. I went to work at WBZ. I was in a job placement program called Project Transition from the Navy, which got me to Boston (from his home in Wisconsin) and a temporary job at WBZ radio. WBZ basically had me doing anything they wanted. Later I was hired full time.

"We had a record room and it was in absolute chaos. We could never find a record when we wanted it, so Dave Maynard came up with the idea of putting me to work in there. Dave said, 'Let's have this kid organize it.' So that's what I did. I was required to come in from nine to five. I was really there from seven to six and didn't care because I was in a 50,000-watt radio station, working in radio, which was my dream.

"I did well, and they felt obligated to help me out anyway they could. So, they called me into Bob Oakes' office, he was the Program Director at the time, he said that I was doing a great job and that they loved everything I was doing. He asked, 'What can we do for you, what are your hobbies?' I said sports, and of course 'BZ was the king of sports at the time. So Bob said to come back at 5 o'clock that afternoon. When I did, he said, 'How would you like to be the statistician for the New England Patriots, the Boston College Eagles, for the Boston Bruins, and the

Boston Celtics. They set it all up and I said I was game. So that's how my connection to the Patriots and obviously Gil came about. Gil became my mentor because my aspirations were in broadcasting. He taught me everything that I know as far as how to broadcast a game, paint the scene, and so on.

"I worked with him from 1971 to 1979. I also hosted *Calling All Sports,* I replaced Bob Lobel and Upton Bell at WBZ. I did that, and as luck would have it in the course of three months 'BZ lost the rights to the Patriots, Celtics, and the Bruins. Bob Oakes felt there was no need to have sports talk radio anymore so that job was gone too.

"So, after WBZ was out of the sports broadcasting business, Gil recommended me to work for NBC. I worked for NBC for the next three years, and worked with every announcing team that came through Foxboro. Through those years, Gil and I remained the best of friends. In 2000, the statistician he had decided to retire and Gil called me and asked me if I wanted to come back to the booth—and here we are with WBCN now.

"We invented the stat board in 1971. It has pretty much every statistic that you could think of that goes on during the course of a game. We've adjusted it here and there over the years but basically it's the same board we used in 1971. When I came back in 2000, I asked, 'What have you got now that works better?' I explained my board again to him because it had been a lay-off of about 14 years, and he said, 'I haven't found anything that works better'—so we put it back in place and have been using it ever since.

"Gino doesn't rely on me as much—Gino is much more independent. He may ask me for things like the yardage and hang time on a punt occasionally but he has his own game-day breakdowns, he has his own notes, and he has his magazines that he uses to fill in his own information. He does all that for the pregame. He is also responsible for reporting halftime stats, and he'll add in a few things for the postgame. Gino's just responsible for his segments and he works on that during the week, so he kind of has that all filled in."

On a single piece of paper, Gino places the names of each player in the relative position where he would line up—just like the X's and O's a coach would draw out on a locker room chalkboard. The starter's name is at the top of each grouping, the second stringer is next, and so on. He supplements this charting system with the game date roster provided by the Patriots management to all broadcasters and reporters covering the game. That 11 x 14 inch poster board chart has a numerical listing and an alphabetical listing of each team on one side, the starting lineups, the names of the officials for the game, and a pronunciation key for some of the more difficult or unusual player names (example: Stephen Gostkowski...gust-OW-ski) on the other. At some point, just before the kickoff, a Patriots employee from the media relations department will enter the booth to inform the broadcasters of "scratches" from the day's lineup. Today it is not just any employee; it is Stacey James, Patriots Vice-President of Media Relations, who checks in with the WBCN team and the network television team next door.

The radio broadcast booth is one of several located just above the first tier of seats at midfield on the south, or "visitors," side of the stadium. The original plans for Gillette Stadium called for the press boxes to be located much higher—enclosed in the southeast corner just under the upper tier of seats even with the far end zone. "The members of the press got involved after seeing the plans for the new stadium and asked that the placement of the booths be changed," according to Gino. "That's why the booths are accessible right from the main concourse where the refreshment stands for the fans are located. It was a last-minute adjustment to the design."

The front of the booth features a folding 4-foot high, 12-foot long window but remains an open-air affair for Gil and Gino despite the severe weather conditions they have encountered over the years—including the coldest game in team history at 4 degrees above zero (a 17–14 victory over Tennessee on January 10, 2004), and the many memorable "Snow Bowl" games in Foxboro. Santos asks, "How can you call a game if you can't feel or experience what the fans in the stadium and the players on the field are going through?" Gino commented, "Years ago at the start of the first game that Gil and I did together in really cold weather—I can't recall exactly when—I went to close the windows when Gil insisted that we needed them open to 'feel the game.' I said as a player and coach 'I've *felt* enough cold, wet or windy games...and I don't want to feel them that way any more if I can help it!'" with a grin on his face. Recalling the final outcome of that little debate over shutting the windows Gino continued, "but Gil is the play-by-play announcer—he is the boss, so the windows stayed open, and have ever since."

Statistician Homan, who shares the front row perch and who has his seat between Gil and Gino, readily agrees with Gino's take. "Gil's the boss, that's what it comes down to. We have known it from day one—there is no surprise. If it were ever going to be closed, it would have been closed in 2004 in the Tennessee playoff game where game time temperature was four degrees—not counting any wind chill so if that game didn't have the windows closed they never will be. I just try to keep my fingers warm so I can write. Because if I can't feel my fingers, I can't write the numbers legibly."

A plastic laminate counter runs the width of the window and electronic microphone gear is secured to it with duct tape. Should anything fall off the 18-inch wide counter, it would drop right on the heads of the fans in the upper reaches of section 131 who are within just a few feet of the booth's open window. Gil, Gino, and statistician Homan position themselves behind the front counter while engineer Dennis Knudsen is behind them to the right on a raised platform with a second counter that forms another few auxiliary broadcasting stations.

As it gets closer to game time, the activity outside the booth increases. The vendors, ushers, security staff, and a legion of uniformed State Police officers and police from scores of cities and towns assemble and take their positions as the stands begin to fill up during the pregame workouts of the Patriots and Redskins. The smell of grilled food permeates the air—hot dogs, sausages, fried chicken, and (only in New England) fried clams and steaming clam chowder.

It is a beautiful fall day in New England. The sky is a bright robin's egg blue without a cloud in sight after a stormy and windy night. Colorful autumn leaves still cling to most of the trees around the stadium, accentuated by a strong October afternoon sun, bringing the temperature at kickoff to a pleasant 60 degrees, but with strong gusting winds still blowing from the west that will last through the first quarter of the game before dying down.

Marc Cappello, the WBCN producer of the game's broadcast, enters the booth with a pigskin covered briefcase—it looks like a big, misshapen football—stuffed with notes, cue cards, and sundry other documents he will refer to constantly throughout the game. His duties include not only the actual game broadcast but also the pre and post game shows from the WBCN "Broadcast Palace" tent located outside of the stadium. It will be a long day for Marc.

He walked into the booth almost unnoticed, as everyone else was concentrating on his own job as the clock wound down to kickoff time. Marc takes what will be his game-time position and stands directly behind the announcers in the narrow space between them and the raised counter where the engineers' equipment rests and starts to unpack his case. He places silver spring-loaded clamps about 6 inches long—the kind of clamps you would use on a woodworking project—on the leading edge of the rear counter. But instead of using the business end of the clamp for his purposes, he uses the vinyl covered handles of the clamps as a resting place or holder for a couple of dozen 6 x 11-inch cue cards that are laminated in plastic. Marc intently continues his pregame routine, tacking some information he needs to keep handy on the bulletin board mounted on the left hand wall of the booth. Next, he places printouts of the commercials and their order of mention on the counter along with a fine point marker he will use to check off each one as it is read. Finally, he grabs his headset and microphone for a transmission check before he looks up and, finally, relaxes for a moment acknowledging and greeting everyone in the booth with a big smile and friendly hello.

"Gil, Gino, and I are the only three members of the entire broadcast team who have been part of the WBCN broadcast since 1994 when the station got the deal. I'm proud of that fact," said Cappello. "I believe that is one of the main reasons why we work so well together. All three of us know each other so well, it makes it so much easier to work. It's almost like during the broadcast, we know what each other is thinking without saying a word—if that makes any sense."

It is almost game time. The 68,756 fans in attendance are in a jubilant mood anticipating not only a Patriots victory this afternoon but also a Red Sox World Series sweep of the Colorado Rockies later on in the evening (the Boston baseball team did, of course, fulfill that destiny and won their *second* World Series Championship in four years after the infamous drought of 86 years without one). It is a banner autumn for New England sports fans—even the Boston College football team has gotten off to its best start and its highest national ranking in history.

Producer Cappello is a bundle of nervous energy standing behind his broadcast team. He sways from side to side, shifting his weight from leg to leg and alternatively pacing in the narrow space. Marc not only has to watch the game but also to communicate with the studio engineers alerting the announcers to breaks for studio broadcast commercials and commercial and programming announcements that have to be made by Gil or Gino from the booth. Hands folded across his chest, he yells out,

"One minute...one minute!" One minute until show time. Marc is a man who is comfortable when he can control the routine of the broadcast. Mark is a bit superstitious as well. "I always wear a sweater-vest on game day. It's a thing I've done since the Super Bowl season in 2001. I did it because as long as they were winning during the regular season I was going to wear one. After winning the Super Bowl after the 2001 season, how could I stop the following seasons?"

A contingent of the Boston Pops Orchestra takes its place on the field and opens the game with a stirring rendition of the National Anthem. Then Gil Santos starts the broadcast by welcoming the listeners, and then Gino introduces the starting lineups. Having set the stage, Santos "throws" to Gino with a statement about the 35-year drought the Patriots have suffered against the Redskins. Cappelletti catches the cue and begins his insightful comments on today's game. "The record between these two teams is somewhat misleading because the Patriots have only faced the Redskins seven times and just three times since 1990. So the win-loss record is somewhat deceiving." A discussion ensues between the two veteran broadcasters and is shared by thousands of fortunate listeners. It seems to be simply a casual chat about football between two old friends—and it is. It is also a conversation between two of the most knowledgeable observers of the game ever to sit behind a microphone.

As the game gets underway with the opening kickoff, Gil calls the play by play. He and Gino are totally concentrated on the action, looking through their binoculars, although often that is not necessary as the players are often within a good viewing distance of the well-placed broadcast booth.

Marc Cappello gives Santos a laminated cue card for a break announcement. Santos reads this and other commercial "copy" with the practiced ease of the experienced broadcaster that he is. Frequently he will hand the copy back to producer Cappello as he is still finishing off the final sentences of the announcements. This time Santos reads the words: "With the score at Foxboro zero to zero we will take a break on the WBCN Rock Radio Network." Gil and Gino then relax a bit and turn their concentration away from the field and into the booth for some good-natured conversation with the rest of the crew. Lots of joking and collegiality is evident on this Sunday afternoon.

Back to the action, Gil sets the scene for his radio audience. His deep baritone voice is modulated and is slightly raspy, giving his words authority. The amount of information he conveys before the play begins is amazing. He paints a mental picture so precise it is no wonder that so many fans find it preferable to listen to him describe the action than to hear any "out of town" television network announcers call the game. Fellow WBCN sports show host Gary Tanguay commented, "Gil Santos gets more good, accurate, information in before the snap of the ball than any other play by play announcer in football."

Santos' deliberate and measured delivery before the play begins often gives way to a very excitable and dramatic recitation of events as the play unfolds. He has the enviable ability to get the audience appropriately excited, but without resorting to the histrionics and hyperbole common to many announcers. Gil continues his portrait of the game with effective descriptive details on every run, pass, tackle, interception, field goal, or action on the field. Players "fall," "dive," "reach," "stretch," "grasp," "leap," "lunge," "tangle," "collide," and "crash."

Between the plays, and sometimes only after several plays have elapsed, Gino may comment. He seems in no rush to be on the air or to make a comment just to be heard. It might be on the previous play, the series of plays, the game's progress, or on any relevant situation he deems important. When he speaks, it is always germane to the action or situation. His comments are conveyed to Gil in a relaxed fashion. It is a very interesting, low-key, and well-informed conversation that is shared with the listeners.

Many times the opportunity for Gino to comment on a play is dictated by the flow of the action on the field. "Gil has the main responsibility to report on the action—set up the plays, and describe them to the audience. I try to be careful not to interrupt Gil's delivery of that important information as he creates that picture with his words. Besides, it is the game that is the entertainment, not us. Sometimes I have to hold back on a comment that I wanted to make because the action in the game might be too rapid for me to get a word in before the next play—say on a no-huddle drive down the field, or at times during a two-minute drive. I may have wanted to say something about a particular play or something but a couple of plays go by and the comment might not be relevant then. I sometimes have to let a lot go."

There is never any hint of one of the broadcasters trying to dominate the mike or verbally stepping on each other. Both men, should they occasionally be inaccurate with a fact or make an erroneous statement, are quick to acknowledge it with a simple "Yes, you're right," or "I didn't realize that." Egos are not an issue.

The Patriots drive 90 yards for a touchdown on the opening drive—Patriots 7, Redskins 0. High fives are rendered all around the booth—the WBCN broadcast team members are also enthusiastic Patriots fans.

With a break in the action, Gino comes back on with the out of town scores from the early games. The Patriots drive again and this time it is a second quarter touchdown pass to linebacker Mike Vrabel, playing on offense as an eligible receiver, a play used often by the Patriots. An observer might think by now that when Vrabel is in the game as an eligible receiver, it would be an obvious give-away to the opposition that the throw will be to him. But even telegraphing the play, Brady hits Vrabel in the end zone for the score. Santos notes, "This catch for Mike Vrabel is his tenth career reception, and is also his tenth touchdown. He has made a touchdown every time he has caught a pass!" New England 14, Washington 0.

Shortly after the Vrabel score and with 5:43 to play in the first half, the Patriots add a Steven Gostkowski field goal to make it 17–0. As the two-minute warning approaches, producer Marc Cappello starts pacing again in the barely adequate walking space between the bulletin boards, the engineer's console, and his announcers.

The Patriots force a Washington fumble with just 1:49 to go in the half and take over the ball on their own 25 yard-line. Santos calls the play and is very animated to say the least. After a few unsuccessful plays, Brady appears to spike the ball to stop the clock with 17 seconds left in the half. The "spike" is a fake and Brady instead throws a 73-yard touchdown pass to Randy Moss to end the half. Santos calls the play. He is *very* excited. Gino, just as thrilled to witness such a great play, maintains his customary composure and analyzes the play with great admiration for Brady, Moss, and the Patriots coaching staff for making the call. Patriots 24-Redskins 0.

At halftime everyone takes a break. Outside of the WBCN booth, there is a table set up with hot and cold drinks and boxed lunches for all of the broadcast teams covering the game. The Fox television team, the NFL film crew, the Patriots in-house film team, as well as the Redskins radio announcers, and others join the 'BCN broadcast team at the smorgasbord. About a dozen hot pizzas are also brought into the booth for snacking throughout the half and the rest of the game.

The home team continues its excellent game plan in the next half. New England scores another unanswered touchdown with 7:14 gone in the third period. It is now 31–0 Patriots. Less than two minutes later, the Patriots recover a Washington fumble and go on to score again. The rout is on with the score 38–0.

Gil and Gino comment on the incredible season thus far, noting that in all seven previous games the Patriots have scored an amazing 30 or more points. In fact, they realize that a new NFL record has been established. The Patriots have scored 30 or more points in nine consecutive games, going back to the AFC Championship game loss against the Colts last season. Today marks the eighth this season.

In the fourth quarter, darkness begins to fall outside Gillette Stadium but inside the fans and field are awash in light from the powerful lighting array on top of the stands. The lights had been on for a while but gradually, almost unnoticed, took over the illumination of the game.

Gillette Stadium is now a bowl of light and noise. The temperature begins to drop rapidly with the absence of the October sun, and wind once again begins to swirl in Foxboro. Santos and Cappelletti are still intently focused on the game. Sitting in their swivel office chairs they have their Sony headsets with attached microphones on their heads. Foam windscreens are taped in place over the mouthpieces. A glittering oversized Super Bowl ring (one of three he has earned during his time as a member of the Patriots family) adorns Gil's right hand as he grasps his binoculars. A burning unfiltered cigarette between his fingers. It is 2007, but for some reason at that moment it feels like a night in 1960.

With nine minutes and five seconds to go in the game, the Patriots score again. New England 45, Washington 0.

By this point in the season the hullabaloo that surrounded the Patriots and the "Spygate" controversy had largely faded away in the minds of Patriots fans. But the "cheating" whine would be brought up in desperation by opposing fans for the rest of the season, through the playoffs, and long after the final whistle of the 2008 Super Bowl.

By this point, it could clearly be seen that the Patriots were an awesome and very talented team that needed no assistance off the field to supplement their on-field prowess. In the first seven games of the season, the team won by scores of: 38–14, 38–14, 38–7, 34–13, 34–17, 48–27, and 48–28. However, rather than laud the Patriots, many members of the national media, and the media in opposing cities had began a new cry against the Pats—that New England was now running up the scores!

In the Patriots' broadcast booth Gil Santos addressed the latest criticism of the Pats. "The Patriots are simply *a great offensive team* is the consensus, perhaps one of the greatest ever to take an NFL field." To emphasize that, Santos noted to his audience that "the Patriots have not only scored 45 points so far in this game, but they have also made 32 first downs today, and that is a new team record." Gino comments in agreement and then reads the rest of the out of town scores of the other late games.

As if to blunt the recent press accusations of running up the scores, Belichick inserts back-up quarterback Matt Cassel into the game. With 5:55 left and the Patriots deep in Washington territory Cassel tries to throw a pass, but all of his receivers are covered. Then, almost apologetically, he runs 15 yards around the right side untouched and scores.

Finally, with just three minutes to play, Washington got their only score of the day and the game ended 52 to 7. Right until the final whistle, producer Cappello remained intently focused on the game as he simultaneously prepared for the postgame show with host Gary Tanguay, who will be joined by the gregarious Andy Gresh and former Pats quarterback Scott Zolak as commentators.

Gil gives the game summary, read from notes prepared on 3 x 5-inch cards by Roger Homan. Santos throws to Cappelletti for the final words on the game. The two men turn in their chairs, face each other, and have a conversation between themselves about the just-completed football game. It is a dialogue *between* the two men, two veteran football announcers, but it is also a conversation *for* the thousands of faithful fans and listeners who choose to hear the "accounts and descriptions" of Patriots football from Gil and Gino this, and every game day.

9

INDIANAPOLIS SHOWDOWN

"Gil Santos' voice will live forever on all those NFL highlight films. I was privileged to work with Gil at WBZ and he is one of the best in the business. Gino is an incredible color guy, so smooth and knowledgeable. What a team." —**LEN BERMAN**, NBC SPORTS

November 4, 2007 at Indianapolis:
New England Patriots 24, Indianapolis Colts 20

Before the Indianapolis Colts game, the Patriots had dominated all eight of their other opponents with an explosive offense, one of record proportions. However, this game, as expected, would prove to be the biggest challenge to the Patriots' offensive dominance thus far in the season. It was the first meeting in the history of the National Football League of teams bearing records of seven or more wins without a loss.

Before the spotlight turned fully to the match of the unbeatens, the spurious charge that the Patriots were deliberately running up the scores to humiliate their opponents continued to be heard from national network commentators, on sports talk radio shows, and ran rampant on the internet blogs.

After the Washington blowout, the simmering criticism of the Pats boiled over. The response to the "running-it-up" argument, by most knowledgeable sports fans, was that it was never the obligation of the winning team to lay down or back off their game in deference to an opponent—especially at the professional level. Rather, it was the obligation of the other team to stop the opposition from scoring and to field a competitive enough team to do just that.

Gil Santos had heard enough of this criticism. In a radio commentary on October 30, following the Redskins game he said, "The national media's obsession and genuine dislike of the Patriots and Bill Belichick continues to hit new and more strident lows as the Pats have cruised unbeaten through their first eight games of the season, outscoring their opponents by a whopping 41–16 *average* score. The whining and outcry of running it up are getting louder with each and every passing game.

"The same people who jumped all over Belichick for the Cameragate business (ignoring the fact that most other teams did it in some way, too) are now piling on Belichick and the Pats for, in their opinion, 'piling it on.' Well, I for one could care less what those Bozos think and I'm very much enjoying the Patriots crush team after team. You see, I have a rather unique perspective on this since I have been broadcasting Patriots games for 31 years now. I have seen them play in over 500 games in person, at home and on the road and I remember quite vividly some of the beatings the Patriots took in the bad old days before they became an NFL power. Let me recall and recite a few.

"In the 30-plus category try 35 to 0, 35 to 7, 33 to 3, 37 to 3.

"On to the 40 point losses: 48–14, 44–16, 41–10, 45–7 (twice), 41–3 45–7, 41–7 (twice), 41–10, 46–10 when the Bears let defensive lineman and overweight "Refrigerator" Perry run one in late in the game [in the 1986 Super Bowl], an ultimate slap in the face then just for the heck of it.

"How about those unbeaten Dolphins of 1972 beating the Patriots senseless 52–0? I didn't hear any whining about teams running it up on the Pats then, but now the John Claytons, Mike Florios, and Mike Freemans of the world, among others, are ripping the Pats for scoring too many points.

"How about telling the defenses they're facing to do something highly unconventional, like tackle them or stop them. What a bunch of whining losers!"

As the Patriots started their incredible season, another team in town was finishing up an equally fantastic year. The Red Sox had just done it again—won their second World Championship in four years by sweeping the Colorado Rockies in four games. The final game of the Series took place on October 28, the same day the Pats had crushed the Washington Redskins at Gillette Stadium in Foxboro.

It was a pretty good time to be a New England fan.

Just after the Washington game and immediately before the Colts game, Santos had this additional comment, "With . . . the Red Sox second World Series title in four years behind us, all attention now focuses on the unbeaten Patriots and their point-scoring machine going into Indi-

anapolis to play the—also unbeaten and also point-scoring machine—
Colts. The Pats are 8–0, the Colts 7–0. It's the first time in NFL history
dating back more than 80 years that two unbeaten teams have clashed
head-on this far into the regular season.

"The Patriots have been destroying their opponents by an average of
25 points per game with some of the nation's media castigating the Pats
for what they term 'running up the score.' I find that pure hogwash.

"The Colts have been beating up their opponents by an average of 17
points per game but somehow to some of the media folks, that's okay because the Colts represent good and the Patriots represent evil. Amazing,
isn't it, that a team that was once laughed at by the same people are now
hated because they are *too good*? Anyway be that as it may, I submit the
Patriots will be the team that comes out of Indy still unbeaten."

Gil's prediction came true but not easily. For most of the game—a re-
match of the 2006 AFC title game that Indy won—it appeared the Colts
would triumph again. The Pats had lost to them three times in succes-
sion and, though the Colts were minus injured star receiver Marvin Harrison and three other starters, they were rolling behind Peyton Manning
with the Pats contributing uncharacteristic mistakes.

Trailing the Colts late in the contest in an extremely noisy and highly
partisan indoor arena—the RCA Dome—the Pats had to muster a dramatic late-game rally to overcome a 20–10 fourth quarter deficit, to win
24–20.

Santos observed: "This is the first game this season that the Patriots
didn't score on their first possession." Defensive linemen Robert Mathis
and Dwight Freeney crashed through to sack Brady, giving the Colts excellent field position, and then Vinatieri (the former Patriots' record setting place-kicker) followed an earlier missed 50-yard field goal (tipped
by Seymour) by connecting this time from 21 for a 3–0 edge.

Then Brady and the Patriots heated things up. He hit Moss for their
12th touchdown connection of the season, a four-yarder that enabled
Moss to tie Stanley Morgan's single-season club record set in 1979 and
Brady to match Vito "Babe" Parilli's franchise mark of 31 touchdown
completions in a season, set in 1964. And this was only Moss's ninth
game. The catch was merely a prelude to an eye-popping one-handed,
leaping 18-yard grab of a Brady missile in the third quarter, one of eight
Moss grabs this day. Naturally, Santos and Cappelletti raved with well
deserved superlatives.

After Vinatieri connected once again for the Colts, this time from

25 yards out, it seemed the Pats would at least have the 7–6 halftime lead until slippery Joseph Addai broke free for a 73-yard catch-and-run touchdown just 13 seconds before intermission. So it was the Colts who enjoyed the halftime lead, 13–7. "The Patriots are missing tackles all over the field," Santos declared to his listening audience. "Addai ran by at least four Patriot defenders." Addai enjoyed a field day, rushing for 112 yards on 26 thrusts and catching five Manning tosses for another 114.

When the Pats went 3-and-out on their initial second-half series, Santos acknowledged their frustration after dominating so many games. "They're staggering right now," he said and Gino agreed. Gino cited "terrible tackling" as Addai ran away again. Still, Stephen Gostkowski's 34-yard field goal lifted the Pats within three, 13–10 entering the fourth quarter.

It appeared the Colts were taking control again when Brady, who had not been intercepted through 175 passes, threw his second of the game, a juggling steal by Gary Brackett. Cappelletti said Matt Light "let his emotions get carried away" with an un-sportsmanlike conduct penalty after the play that left the Colts at the Patriot 32. Sure enough: Manning capped a short drive as he scored from a yard out and Indy had a 20–10 command with 9:42 left.

The Pats then rallied on a second straight Brady-to-Wes Welker toss, for a touchdown, coming from three yards with 7:59 to go, despite having to overcome what most observers agreed was an earlier phantom offensive pass interference call against Moss, who had already caught six straight Brady aerials. The Indy lead was 20–17.

When Peyton Manning could not get the Colts moving again, it took Brady just 43 seconds to engineer a decisive drive—finding Moss for five yards, Donte Stallworth for 33 and Kevin Faulk for a 13-yard touchdown that completed the stirring comeback—a 24–20 victory.

Where the Patriots had faded against the Colts in the 2006 AFC championship game, they came on magnificently this time. "They scored two touchdowns in the last five minutes," Santos pointed out. "Brady has 33 touchdown passes, a team record, and the defense really came together in the fourth quarter." Gino chimed in: "Just when everything wasn't going their way, they got going. Brady had great passes to Moss and Stallworth, putting the ball right where it had to be."

When the chips were down, here came Tom Brady and his 25th career comeback victory, whizzing passes downfield to the incredible

Randy Moss, the speedball Donte Stallworth, and the irrepressible streak that is Wes Welker, and suddenly in a span of five minutes, from the eight-minute mark left in the game to the three, the Patriots came back to win.

So the Patriots entered their bye-week as the NFL's only undefeated team, 9–0. "Through those nine games, everyone was marveling about Brady, Moss, Wes Welker, and Donte Stallworth, but the defense was not getting enough credit because the offense was running up big scores," Santos said.

The victory made the Patriots the sole unbeaten team in the NFL, and gave new relevance to Richard Seymour recalling Tedy Bruschi's flashback to the Pats' 21-game winning streak that capped the 2003 super-season. Seymour declared to the *Boston Globe*: "I think Tedy said it best: 'We won 21 games in a row, but we did it one at a time. We won one game 21 times in a row. That's how we look at it.'"

So Seymour did not address growing speculation of a perfect season. No one in the Patriots organization did. Not yet. Not with nearly a half-season left, even though future foes did not seem capable of overcoming Brady's bunch. But Santos did have this to say: "The win in Indianapolis showed how this team would react in a tight game. They were behind, 20–10, against Dallas earlier this season. The Patriot defense shut Dallas down in the fourth quarter. And they won, 24–20. before this game the Colts had been averaging 35 points a game and the Patriots held them to 20 at their home arena."

Playing and beating an opponent, especially a very good opponent, at their home field is always a daunting assignment, particularly if the home field is housed in an enclosed arena like the RCA Dome, where the noise of the partisan crowd is trapped and enhanced by the roof. It is especially tough for the visiting signal-caller to be heard at the line of scrimmage over the screams of thousands of frenzied home fans.

An unusual audio moment, heard by millions, occurred during the CBS television broadcast of the Patriots-Colts game in the Dome. At one point, the incredibly loud crowd noise seemed to "skip," just like an old phonograph record sometimes did or as a faulty CD does if scratched or dirty. The accusation was quickly made that the Colts were using their public address system to record and then amplify and play back the crowd noise into the Dome to enhance the actual live noise.

The incident was quickly dubbed "Noisegate" and just as quickly dismissed by the NFL brass who decided that the "skipping" crowd noise was in some way just a technical problem in the CBS broadcast audio and was not heard or transmitted into the Dome.

Patriots fans remained skeptical but were happy to walk away with the victory. Gil commented, "Oh, that incredible noise in the Indy Dome? Do I think it was enhanced? Of course I do—but it really didn't matter."

It was midseason and the Patriots were on an unprecedented journey, but the controversies surrounding the team—distractions from outside elements—would not abate. First the video issue raised by Mangini of the Jets tried to suggest that the Pats could not win fair and square. Then after they demonstrated their dominance of opponents game after game they were bashed for being too good. Then they were questioned as to their ability to win a close one—which was answered in convincing and dramatic fashion in hostile Indianapolis, "Noisegate," or no "Noisegate."

Perhaps the most annoying distraction that surfaced was the unwarranted and controversial statement of former Miami Dolphins head coach and Hall of Famer Don Shula following the Patriots' hard-won victory in Indianapolis. With each victory of the Patriots, the threat to Shula's 1972 Dolphins remaining the only unbeaten team in NFL history became more and more ominous.

Shula and the members of that 1972 undefeated Dolphin team have jealously guarded their place in football history ever since. It is said that every year since the 1972 season ended a bottle of chilled champagne kept in the Dolphins owners' stadium suite is broken open, with the coach and members of the team present, each time that the remaining undefeated team of the present season loses. The Dolphins have a champagne toast—a toast to their own record, and to celebrate the first loss of the team that may be challenging it in any given year.

Gino Cappelletti recalled just how far the members of that 1972 Dolphins' organization would go to protect their legacy. "The 1985 Chicago Bears were 12–0 when they went to Miami to play the Dolphins. That whole '72 Dolphins team lined up behind the Dolphins bench and made themselves very visible, made their presence known to the players on the field. All of the younger Miami players knew *why* the '72 guys were there. They were trying to inspire, and also to somewhat intimidate the team. And sure as hell they did—they knocked off the undefeated Bears that year."

It was the only game the Bears lost in 1985. They finished the season at 18–1 including a victory over the wild card New England Patriots in the 1986 Super Bowl—Super Bowl XX.

When Shula was asked if he thought the Patriots could become the first team since his Dolphins to go undefeated in the regular season and through the playoffs to win the Super Bowl, he said, "Yes, they could." But his comment did not end there; he added that because of the Cameragate/Spygate controversy at the start of the season, if they went 19–0, they should have an asterisk placed next to their record.

A "totally unnecessary caveat," according to Gil Santos when he heard of Shula's remarks. Santos went on to comment, "On hearing that remark by Shula, I thought of a movie preview I saw a couple of weeks ago where someone said to Jack Nicholson, 'You know what I think?' and smiling Jack says, 'No one cares what you think!' And that's how I feel. I don't care what Don Shula thinks. Yes, he was a great coach. Yes, his 1972 team was an unprecedented 17–0, and no team has been able to go through an NFL season unbeaten since then.

"That being said, let me point out a few items of comparative interest. The '72 Dolphins played in an era when there were no salary cap restrictions, nor was there free agency—unlike today. In '72 the Dolphins played exactly four games against teams that had a winning record the year before. This season, the Patriots are playing ten games against teams that had winning records! They're playing seven teams that were in the postseason. The '72 Dolphins played [just] three playoff teams in their regular season run. And as far as running up the scores, the '72 Dolphins beat the '72 Patriots 52–0!"

After analyzing the differences and the relatively harder circumstances the Patriots faced in creating a championship team year after year, Santos had this to say about the knock against the Pats. "So Don Shula, I don't care what you think since you are clearly someone trying to protect his legacy, and that's fine. Just don't try to taint what this team may do. Oh, and by the way, can you name an NFL team and coach that had to give up a first-round draft pick because they were caught cheating? Why, the Dolphins and Don Shula!—because he was still the head coach of the Baltimore Colts in 1969 when he signed to coach Miami and Miami was charged with tampering by the NFL!"

Despite all the off-field distractions, the Patriots remained a strong and cohesive organization—the critics and the criticism only seemed to strengthen their resolve. All for one, and one for all, was no hackneyed expression for this team—it was the Patriots' way of doing business.

Jimmy Johnson succeeded Shula as the Miami head coach in 1996. Now with Fox television sports, he supported Gil's reasoning regarding the Patriots' achievements in 2007–2008 compared to that of the Dolphins in 1972–1973. "I think the Patriots are by far the best team in the NFL since the salary cap and free agency. But one reason you can't compare before that is because teams used to stockpile talent. The reason they're the best is Belichick is an outstanding coach. He coaches new players, young players, rookies, and free agents and then on top of that, he coaches the coaches. He lost Charlie Weis (to Notre Dame), Romeo Crennel (to Cleveland) and Eric Mangini (to the Jets). What does he do? He grooms young coaches to take their place."

The Patriots could finally rest a bit in their attempt to forge an historic season—a week off in their schedule was next. It was their NFL bye week and was chance to regroup from their rugged schedule and from the many off-the-field controversies the media seemed intent on manufacturing.

10

ON THE ROAD AGAIN

"I know Gil is one of the best football announcers. In fact, of all the radio guys I've ever heard, going back to Bill Stern and Harry Wismer, Gil's as good as I've ever heard. I think Gino was one of the first ex-players to go into color. I wasn't high on some ex-athletes in that role for a long while, but Gino's a very good analyst. He's one reason I've come around to realize an athlete has a lot to offer on the air."—**BOB WILSON**, RETIRED BRUINS HALL OF FAME RADIO VOICE

November 18, 2007 at Buffalo:
New England Patriots 56, Buffalo Bills 7

The bye week could not have come at a better time for the Patriots. After a grueling nine games, each one getting tougher and tougher, the team needed some rest. A week off was just the thing needed, to regroup and prepare for the next game and final seven games of the regular season.

Although they had defeated the Bills handily at Gillette stadium in game three of the season, playing the archrival Bills in the second half of the season and in Buffalo was always a difficult task. Although recently the Pats had dominated the Bills (13–2 since 2000), the Patriots acknowledge that it is always a big challenge to win in the cold and windy stadium near Lake Erie. Besides that, the Bills had just recently played the then-undefeated Cowboys very hard in Buffalo. That was a game most observers thought the Bills could have and should have won. The Bills appeared to be a much better team than the one the Patriots defeated in Foxboro at the start of the season.

The trip to Buffalo, like most Patriots road games, started around 11 a.m. on Saturday at Gillette Stadium. As everyone who has traveled by air since 2001 knows, the federal safety regulations governing travel apply to *all* travelers. The rules of the Transportation Security Administration (TSA) apply to everyone—from business people, to vacationers, even to pro football teams. All airline passengers must undergo rigorous security measures by the TSA before being allowed to board a commercial aircraft. The only difference between the Patriots and the rest of the flying public is that most everyone has to go the airport *before* they go through the scrutiny of the TSA. For the Patriots, the airport comes to them.

The TSA and Gillette Stadium security establish a mobile TSA inspection station right in the service entrance area of the stadium. Support personnel, the WBCN radio team including Gil and Gino, and team guests go through security first and are escorted through a cordoned area directly to one of the two, or sometimes three, huge and quite comfortable buses that take them to T. F. Green Airport south of Providence for their charter flight—this time to Buffalo. The first group waits on the buses another hour or so for the coaches and team members to follow. It is a good time for crossword puzzles, a good book, or to watch a video.

Once the team has boarded, the buses convoy down Route 1 to Interstate 95 for the short ride to Warwick and T. F. Green Airport. Once they arrive, the buses drive right onto the tarmac and up to the waiting plane. Again, TSA personnel guide all of the passengers directly from the buses to the charter craft.

After recalling many trips over the years to NFL cities around the country, Gino related how Bill Belichick made life a little more pleasant and comfortable for him and his partner. "During the first year of Bill Belichick's tenure and during the preseason, Gil and I sat in the mid-section of the plane with the other people in the broadcast team for the road games. We all sat together. And then for the regular season, as we were getting on the plane and were looking for our seats—they had names placed on the seats for all the individuals who were flying, whether they were staff people for the radio, which we were, or the staff people employed by the Patriots. As we were looking around for them in the mid-section of the plane the flight attendant said, 'No, you are sitting up in the first class section, you and Gil." I said, 'You're kidding.' We walked up there and sure enough our names were on seats in the first class seats—the first two.

"So, we took off on the first flight of the season in first class and I said to Gil, 'You better hope and pray that we win this game. If we do, we'll be sitting here more often. If we lose, maybe they'll look at it as a bad omen and send us back!' I think it was a nice show of respect to us from Bill for years of service, and Bill has been known to do that. He honors tradition and he honors loyalty and longevity."

Thinking about the plane seating arrangement and some of the traditions or superstitions that teams have, Gil added, "In 2001, with the first Super Bowl championship team, that was the year that we lost the first two games, and were 2–3 by game six. Game six was a road game against the Colts. So when we landed, we get up from our two seats—there are two seats in the middle aisle and then two seats on the other side. Charlie Weis always sat in the aisle seat on the far right aisle. And he was always the first one out the door when we landed.

"We'd get up and Charlie would come around that partition there and he'd go down the stairs first, remember this was a charter flight—no jet way. Instead, there were stairs down to the tarmac and the waiting charter buses. So we get up and have our bags in our hands and Charlie's standing there waiting for the door to open, and he said, 'Gil, you go out first—see if that changes our luck,' so I went out the door first. Well, we actually won that game, 38–17!

"So the next road game we get up to get off the plane, Charlie says, 'Hey, we're not screwing with this. You go first!' So I just kept going out the door first for every road game. So when we got into the playoffs and there were all kinds of people waiting with TV cameras and photographers all over the place ready to shoot Belichick and Brady getting off of the plane, I can imagine them all wondering 'Who the heck is this guy?' As a matter of fact at the last game, a road game at Indy, when we were set to get off the plane, Ivan Fears (running backs coach) was standing by the door and I motioned for him to get off ahead of me. He said, 'No, no, no, no, no!! We've got a good karma thing going here, Gino goes first, you go second, I go third.' So now Gino goes down the stairs first, I go second, and Ivan is right behind me!

"Last year, we went to Indianapolis to play the championship game and I broke a tradition. I always wear the '96 Super Bowl runner-up ring, (much smaller and much less ostentatious than any championship ring). But for that game I decided to wear the third Super Bowl Championship ring—and Marc Cappello our producer said, 'Why are you…you don't have your ring on.' I said, 'No, I have this one.' He said, 'If we lose this game, you are never wearing that ring to another game!' I said, 'OK.' Well, as you know, we lost that game and I have never worn it to a championship game since then. I'm back to my old runner-up ring. I'm not changing it again."

Gino smiled as he heard Gil go on about some of the funny and sometimes unusual superstitions, habits, or rituals that somehow have always been a part of professional sports. "I had them as a player, but I can't really say I've got anything pertaining to what Gil is saying as a broadcaster. I have heard of coaches that have worn the same undershorts for each game. Everybody connected to the game—coaches and players alike—have got some sort of superstition although everyone might not admit to it. But you can talk to the players' wives if you really want to find out about individual superstitions before a game. They will tell you, 'Oh yeah, he wants *those* socks on and he wants this and that is just the way it was the game before'—that sort of thing.

"Me, as a player I had to have pasta before I left home for the game. And I'm talking about 9 o'clock in the morning if it was a home game. I had to have pasta for a number of reasons I guess, because I wanted to and because of the loading up on carbohydrates, and also it's what I liked. Then when I left to go to the stadium, I'd drive a certain way, down Route 9. It was important to me not to change my routine. Then when I got there, I wanted my right ankle taped first instead of my left. And then when I walked out, especially at Fenway Park, when I walked out of the tunnel and when I got to the end of the tunnel before I stepped out of the dugout to go out on the field, I would tap my kicking toe into a certain section of the wall there, because I had a square toe. When you think of some of the gear we had to wear in those days, it didn't help your speed, those Riddell shoes were heavy. Anyway, I was popping it, making it nice and tight. And then I would go out and I'd stand by a goal post to hold myself onto it and I would stretch out one way and then stretch out the other. That was it."

After landing in Buffalo, the trip for the Patriots and their entourage continued with a short ride in another set of large, well-appointed charter buses, which took the team to the Adam's Mark Hotel on the shore of Lake Erie. The hotel is about a half-hour ride from the suburban town of Orchard Park where Ralph Wilson Stadium is located.

Every time the team is on the road, Gil and Gino, Roger, and Marc dine together at one of their favorite restaurants. This trip, the quartet spent a quiet evening at one of their favorite Western New York restaurants relaxing before the game. "Wherever we go, we usually have a favorite restaurant," confirmed Gil. "When Gino is finished with his weekly interview with Bill, we have already made our reservations, go out, and have a nice dinner. We come back, relax, and go to sleep, do the game the next day."

On the road, Gino does his pregame interview with the coach the night before the game and tapes it. At home he does it live just before the game on the WBCN pregame show.

"Yes," Gino added. "When we arrive at the hotel, they have the TV production meeting with the network, in this case NBC, scheduled when they arrive. The first thing they do, Bill goes right to Madden and Al Michaels. Sometimes he'll do his interview with me first if they are late or something—or I'll wait for them to finish, then we can relax a bit and go enjoy that fine meal together."

The game, originally slated for an early afternoon broadcast the next day, was shifted to an 8:15 p.m. start as the *Sunday Night Football* offering in order to accommodate the continually growing national interest in the Patriots and their undefeated record.

Prime time television was starting to become a weekly event for the Pats.

Many of the Buffalo fans braved daytime temperatures in the low 30s by tailgating in the parking lots around Ralph Wilson Stadium from before noontime that Sunday. By game time, they were more than primed and ready to see their Bills try to make history against the undefeated Patriots.

The WBCN broadcast technicians and engineers also made an early trip to Orchard Park, at least five hours before kickoff, to set up the broadcast booth and connect with the studio back in Boston. Pretty much the same crew that operates the Gillette Stadium booth goes on the road with the team. The many mixing boards, microphones, cables, connectors, and assorted other electronic gadgets travel to every away game along with the Patriots' equipment—sometimes trucked ahead or flown depending on the venue.

One change in the staffing of the support crew is the head engineer in the booth—the person handling the mixing board and the communication back to the studio in Boston. Joe Soucise, the chief engineer weekdays at sister station WZLX, takes over the controls of every away game instead of Gillette-based Dennis Knudsen. Joe is in his first year as the WBCN road engineer, so he is seeing the stadiums across the NFL for the first time and likes to get to the stadiums well in advance of not only game time, but also the pregame show as well.

The only other change in the usual game-day routine of the WBCN Patriots' "Rock Radio" network is how the pregame, halftime, and postgame shows are done. Gary Tanguay hosts the show along with Andy Gresh. Former Patriots quarterback Scott Zolak and former lineman Pete Brock are the regulars at the "Broadcast Palace" outside of Gillette Stadium when the Pats play at home. But instead of bringing that portion of Patriots coverage on the road, the shows are broadcast directly from the WBCN studios in Brighton, Massachusetts. Patriots Network executive producer Howie Sylvester runs the operation and coordinates the game broadcast from there as it goes out on the 33-station Patriots network.

Like the football team, the Patriots broadcasters and crew all stay in the same facility. In this case as noted, it was the Adam's Mark Hotel in downtown Buffalo—at the most a 20 or 30 minute ride out to Orchard Park and the stadium. However, this time, it seemed that Joe Soucise and the rest of the technicians from WBCN had a little trouble getting there.

"We always try to be at the stadium five hours before the game, so that should have been about 3 p.m. We left the hotel about 2 p.m. to be safe, but due to a cab driver from Buffalo who claimed to be a season ticket holder—but couldn't find Ralph Wilson Stadium, we didn't arrive till nearly 4 p.m.! He had us on a tour of the Western New York countryside as far away as a town called Eden. So we were a bit rushed, to say the least, in getting going. Fortunately, everything was well marked and in close proximity to the board and amazingly everything was working at that time.

"As the game progressed, about the start of the second half, the main telephone circuit to 'BCN kept hanging up on us. So after trying a couple of times to reconnect, it was decided to finish the game on the backup circuit and that was stable for the duration. This was my first time there to Buffalo and also the first time for me to have phone line circuit issues. If the main line to the station fails, they merely fade up the backup line in the Boston studios. We always feed the main and backup lines circuits continuously the same program. The only difference between the two is the main circuit is stereo and the backup circuit is a mono feed.

"Gil and Gino always sound the same, whether we are in stereo or in mono. The difference would be noticed in the background sounds where we feed the crowd microphone in stereo and the parabolic (sideline microphones) come though in stereo."

Two buses shuttle the team, coaches, and support staff to the stadium. One bus leaves for the game with the players whose habit it is to get to the field early, for their own pregame workout routines or for some extra attention from the trainer. The second bus is the one that Gil, Gino, and Roger Homan ride on. It arrives a couple of hours prior to kickoff and the broadcast team has plenty of time to settle into their broadcast location.

Buffalo's stadium may seem familiar to visiting New England fans—if not from being there before then from recognizing that the big bowl has a striking resemblance to the old Schaefer-Sullivan-Foxboro Stadium, once home to the Pats. Although recently renovated, the Buffalo facility dates back to 1973—the same vintage as the Pats' old 1971–2001 home. It has been updated and renovated over the years, most recently this past season. Like the old Foxboro facility, the playing surface is in a scooped-out bowl below ground level and the upper level seats rise high around that bowl in a preformed concrete structure.

To get to the press booth level, Gil and Gino simply walk in from the parking lot—no stairs or elevators needed as the field is spread out some 50 feet below. Originally called Rich Stadium, Buffalo's facility was renamed in honor of the Bills' founder and owner Ralph Wilson in 1998. Walking into the stadium, Gino had a strange feeling of déjà-vu.

Gil suggested that the feeling might be a memory of an unusual incident that took place years before when the stadium was new, and as the two of them made the same walk to the press box entrance. (Rich Stadium replaced the old War Memorial Stadium as the Bills' new home.) "It was the early 1970s and there was this guy in Buffalo who called Gino before the game and had an idea for a food product to sell at the games. It was called a Coni-Roni and it was like an ice cream cone made out of pizza dough or something like that and it was flaky. You'd put a scoop of macaroni with meat sauce in it. He thought this would go over big, especially at cold-weather sites. At stadiums, people could eat a Coni-Roni."

The enterprising Coni-Roni guy had set up a stand outside of the stadium entrance and was giving out free samples to try and test the market

"So they bring us these Coni-Ronis before the game and I said to this guy, 'Is there any cheese in it?' He said, 'Yes.' I said I couldn't eat it because I'm allergic to cheese but Gino eats it and says, 'Oh, this is delicious!' So the game starts and we're at the new stadium in Orchard Park. I'm calling the game in the first quarter and I'm concentrating on the field. Some play happens and I say, 'What did you think of that, Gino?' And I get no response. I said 'Gino' and I turn to look and he's gone. So I ad-lib something, keep going and a little while later, Gino comes back. At the next commercial break I asked, 'What happened? Where were you?'

"He said, 'That bloody Coni-Roni! In five minutes, my stomach started rumbling and bumbling and I knew I couldn't say anything to you. I had to bolt out of here for the bathroom!'"

And so *that* was Gino's first experience, and perhaps his most memorable experience in the then-new Buffalo stadium. Not exactly one of the notable gourmet dining experiences he and Gil are known to talk about as they travel to all the NFL cities around the country!

Although the Buffalo stadium may be suffering a bit as it ages, as did Foxboro Stadium, the Bills management has kept pace with as many improvements as possible, including adding luxury suites, new electronic scoreboards, and a fine upgrade of the press box.

The press box is a two-story, glass-fronted facility above the first level of stadium seating on the home side. It is about 120 feet long and runs from one 30-yard line to the other. The center portion can accommodate nearly 200 reporters and media in four rows of tiered seating—reminiscent of a college lecture hall. Behind the raised seating area is the press lounge where a buffet is offered and refreshments of all kinds are served—but *no* Coni-Roni!

To the right of the center section, there are five smaller glass-walled booths, one for the instant replay officials who rule on challenges to the calls on the field, a multi-purpose booth, the visiting coaches booth, the visiting radio booth, and another booth reserved for Bills guests of all kinds. The television booth with Al Michaels and John Madden calling the game is the first booth to the left of the main pressroom. Then the Bills coaches, the Bills radio announcers, and the scoreboard operators take up the rest of the booths to the left.

The WBCN crew has set up all the electronic gear for the broadcast as Gil and Gino settle in and begin their individual pregame preparation. The booth is much less spacious than the booth in Foxboro. Gil, Roger, and Gino squeeze in, shoulder to shoulder. But the booth does have windows that open! Gil immediately raises the double-hung aluminum-framed glass panels and settles into his seat. Gino and statistician Roger Homan exchange knowing grins on this chilly evening.

Since this booth is situated close to the 35-yard line, Gil and Gino have to look through the glass partition on their left, separating them from the Patriots coaches box to be able to see all of the field and the west end zone. It is a less than ideal situation, but one that can be fairly easily compensated for. That is, until an unusual thing started to happen. Just before kickoff, the Patriots coaches and staff took a bunch of towels, paper, and rolls of duct tape, and proceeded to cover up the glass walls between them and the booths on either side. Within a few minutes, the view of the field to the left was completely obscured by a patchwork of towels, newspapers, and tape. It might be understating things a bit to say that the coaches wanted their privacy. They certainly got it, and as a result, every time Gil or Gino made the call of a play on the far left side, they had to stand up and lean out of the booth window a dozen feet above the crowd below.

Over 70,000 fans filled the Buffalo stadium for the nationally televised November 18 contest. Except for a relatively small contingent of Patriots fans scattered around the park, the large overwhelmingly hometown crowd was hoping for an upset of major proportions.

It was anything but that. The Patriots scored on their first seven possessions. Brady threw four of his five touchdown strikes to Moss, the gap was 35–7 at halftime and the final count was 56–10—the biggest drubbing doled out by the Pats so far. It predictably led to more piling-on charges against the Patriots by the media. Brady broke Steve Grogan's team-record career touchdown passing mark with 185. Moss tied an NFL mark with four first-half touchdown receptions.

Cappelletti exhaled the quote of the night after just 3:43 into the game when Maroney opened the scoring siege with a six-yard run. Gino, realizing the Bills were no match despite entering with four straight wins, commented off the air to Gil and Roger Homan: "It's over already!" He knew!

11

SIX MORE TO PERFECTION

"Santos is a perfect football guy. Football has a rhythm—stop, go into the huddle, play. It's not free flowing like basketball and hockey. I worked with Gil doing college basketball games on Channel 56 back in the 1970s and '80s and I know he's a terrific announcer. Gino is terrific too, providing insight for the listeners who can't see the game. They've been together so long, they can finish each other's sentences."

—**TOM HEINSOHN**, CELTICS HALL-OF-FAME PLAYER, AND TELEVISION BROADCASTER

November 25, 2007 at Foxboro:
New England 31, Philadelphia Eagles 28

Quite often in the NFL, a seeming rout before kickoff turns into a great game. The odds makers in Las Vegas and the pundits in the papers sometimes *really* get it wrong. It did not seem possible that the 5–5 Philadelphia Eagles, underdogs by a heaping 24 points and playing minus star quarterback Donovan McNabb, would give the unbeaten Patriots a strong argument in Foxboro November 25. But they did—and almost won. Santos and Cappelletti were stunned and so was NBC's national TV audience for Al Michaels and John Madden, who had the Patriots game for the second week in a row.

At the start of the Eagles game, a reporter in the WBCN radio booth ran into Al Michaels in the hallway at Gillette as they both stepped out to get a cup of coffee. The reporter related to Michaels how at one point, while up in Buffalo covering the game the week before, his wife called on his cell phone after the third quarter to tell him that, 'Even Al Michaels is finally saying nice things about the Patriots!' as she watched the game back in Boston. Now it is true that Patriots fans can be pretty parochial when it comes to criticizing the national media and announcers. But Michaels had to laugh and say, "Well, it's pretty easy to say nice things about the Patriots when they were winning 42 to 10 at the time!"

As the game unfolded in Foxboro, it was clear that this would not be another rout for the Patriots. For the second time in the season, the Patriots had to rally from behind in the fourth quarter to win. They beat Philly by a mere three points—the same nail-biting three-point margin by which they edged the Eagles for their third Super Bowl victory in 2006. This time, the score was 31–28, but the tense drama was much different than their fourth-quarter comeback that overcame Indianapolis three weeks before.

This time, the Pats' defense was breached—most notably the secondary which was whipped repeatedly by usual backup quarterback A. J. Feeley, whom Santos declared, after the Eagles took a 21–17 lead, was "just shredding the Patriot defense." But Brady, using Wes Welker as his main target for 13 pass connections and 149 yards, rallied the Patriots offense twice to avoid an astounding upset. The win also insured the Patriots' AFC East title with five games to go in the regular season.

As John Madden said on NBC, "In the end what the Eagles did was offer to the rest of the NFL a blueprint on how to beat the Patriots, even though they couldn't finish the job." They harassed Brady with three sacks and four hits. They neutralized Moss by double-covering him. They swarmed over all the Pats receivers except Welker, and their own receivers were repeatedly open."

To counter Madden's assessment, the WBCN duo of Santos and Cappelletti astutely pointed out that cornerback Asante Samuel had major answers—interceptions that Santos observed started and finished the contest with a positive outcome for the now 11–0 Patriots. His pickoff of Feeley and 40-yard touchdown return just 1:22 into the game started what many had to think would be yet another rout. And his end zone interception of an ill-conceived Feeley bomb sealed the Eagles' fate.

It also preserved a Pats' fourth-quarter pattern of not just Brady heroics but defensively stopping a foe in the closing moments. Santos commented at the end of this contest: "With the Patriots remaining undefeated, you can keep those champagne bottles corked in Miami," referring to the 1972 Dolphins and their tradition of celebrating the first loss of any NFL team that threatened their undefeated record.

Santos remarked throughout the broadcast that the Patriots had tried only one running play in the first half—not including a Brady scramble—as Laurence Maroney stayed on the sideline most of the time. But ironically, after Brady hit Jabar Gaffney with his 39th touchdown pass of the season, giving the Pats their 24–21 halftime edge, it was Maroney who made the difference with a four-yard touchdown trot—erasing the

Philly lead that Feeley had provided with an eight-yard touchdown pass to Reggie Brown earlier.

Before that, Santos kept noting the "back-and-forth" nature of this game, surprising after so many lopsided scores of the other Patriots' wins. On NBC, before Maroney's decisive score, Madden noted that the Eagles had to stay aggressive to stay ahead. But Brian Westbrook, usually dependable, dropped what was a second straight Philly incompletion, and Brady had his chance, igniting a 10-play drive toward Maroney's score with 7:20 to play.

"The Patriots showed great poise when they had to have it," Santos lauded. "Welker was the player of the game." Cappelletti jumped in: "Welker brings something we haven't seen in such a long while—such speed! He really got into the right situation here [after being with Miami]. He has great pass-catching talent and a great burst of speed. And the way the Patriots kept moving the ball was important."

No one was speaking of a dynasty after this game—unlike Madden had following the Pats' 46-point margin over Buffalo a week earlier. But with weak opponents ahead, the definite possibility of a perfect season remained. The Patriots had been favored by more than three touchdowns; at least they had averted an incredible upset.

After the game, Gino reacted to the assertion by many pundits that even in its loss, Philadelphia had come up with a plan to stop the Patriots juggernaut. "I don't know. It worked pretty well for them, whatever they did. I don't think anybody can come up with a 'blueprint' as they say to stop the Patriots. You can get an idea of some of the things that worked for them. But they had the players to execute what *they* wanted to do. I think everybody else is going to have to approach *their* game differently with the Patriots.

"You know, each team has certain strengths defensively. Some teams have it in the outside edge, some in the interior, and then of course some teams are better at disguising their front better then others when they are blitzing. The Eagles just came up with a nice plan, and the players really executed it well to cause the Patriots some problems. But again the Patriots were able to overcome it and come up with the scores and then they did it with their own defense as well."

With a Monday night date in Baltimore ahead, Santos kept focusing on the phrase he used to start the Philly game—predicting that the Patriots would "continue their pursuit of perfection on the national stage."

December 3, 2007 at Baltimore:
New England Patriots 27, Baltimore Ravens 24

In the aftermath of the Patriots' apparent difficulties against the Eagles there was much discussion about how Philadelphia "created a blueprint," according to John Madden, on how to defeat New England—if that blueprint is executed successfully. Dan Marino on a CBS broadcast countered that thought this way, "All week long, I'm hearing about how Philly gave the league a blueprint to beat the Patriots. I say they gave them (the Patriots) a blueprint to go undefeated. When you have the resolve of Tom Brady and Bill Belichick and that veteran team, they're going to correct from that tape and find out what they need to go undefeated. Tom Brady: get rid of the football, don't take the sacks and hits. Be more balanced on offense. In my opinion, Philly had their shot. They didn't get it done. New England is going undefeated learning from the game tape."

Over on the Fox network, Howie Long added his thoughts on the subject. "The only person who can stop New England's offense is the guy whose game plan stopped 'The Greatest Show On Turf' in Super Bowl 36 and also the guy whose game plan sits in Canton, Ohio for stopping the Buffalo Bills in Super Bowl 25. That would be Bill Belichick and that's not happening. If this team wins another championship this year, I think you have to mention Belichick and Tom Brady in the conversation for best ever at what they do."

That prediction by Marino may have proven true and the observation by Long right on target, but the Patriots' next foe wasn't going to make it easy for them. Those who thought the closeness of the Philadelphia game was shocking were in for another jolt on December 2, when the unbeaten Patriots hit Baltimore to play the 4–7 Ravens, who had a solid defensive reputation but had seemed lacking on offense. What unfolded before Gil and Gino was a series of stunning developments—including the outcome decided largely by just plain luck.

It was not only that the heavily favored Pats needed a trio of fourth-down tries just to stay alive in the fourth quarter, or that an opposing coach helped the Pats greatly by calling a timeout, or that a "Hail Mary" heave by Ravens quarterback Kyle Boller nearly provided a miracle ending. But also there was a rarity for Santos: as a result of his position in the radio booth, he *couldn't see* Jabar Gaffney snare the winning eight-yard touchdown pass from Tom Brady with just 44 seconds left!

Perhaps if Gil and Gino had some advance idea of what the visiting team radio booth was like they could have prevented what was one of the very few missed calls made in this remarkable season. Perhaps. When asked about the logistics and the situation for the broadcasters in Baltimore before the game, Gino had to say, "I've never been there. This is the first time we are going into this ballpark. The last time we were there we played at Memorial Stadium, but now they have this Bank something [M & T Bank] Stadium right next to Camden Yards. This is our first go in that stadium."

When the WBCN radio team got to the booth, they discovered that it was another new and difficult location to add to their less than ideal list. Santos explained in a postgame interview: "Our location was at about the 35-yard line with the field stretching 65 yards to my left. Unlike Foxboro with the accordion windows, this booth had the pull-up windows with posts on my left, middle, and right. The middle post prevented me from seeing plays between the 45-yard lines, and the TV monitor was above us. So I sat in the left seat and there was a very slim corner of the end zone that I couldn't see—about five yards wide. I figured the odds of a play happening there were very unlikely.

"I saw Brady throw and there was nobody there, so I said the pass was incomplete. I said he threw it away and Gino said, 'No, it's a touchdown!' I said, 'To whom?' He said, 'Gaffney.' I looked up at the monitor and saw Gaffney make the catch right at the very spot I couldn't see. I thought, 'Son of a gun!' Someone said, 'Couldn't you call the play off the monitor?' You can't do that. I'd have to take my eyes off the field and look up at the monitor. It's impossible." But I said, 'I'm gonna hate this window post for the rest of my life! This is the biggest play of the game and I couldn't see it!'"

Then came the official review when it seemed Gaffney juggled the ball, switching hands, as both feet landed clearly in the end zone. On ESPN, Tony Kornheiser and Ron Jaworski, who both seemed to be rooting for an upset of the Pats much of the night, questioned whether Gaffney had possession. But the referee saw the replay and determined that he had, infuriating the Ravens, who thought the officials had peppered them with bad calls.

That sequence was far from the only incredible happening. The Ravens appeared bound for a huge upset through much of the game, including earlier in that decisive series when Brady was stuffed on fourth-and-one at the Baltimore 30 with 1:48 to play. Yet, incredibly, defensive coordinator Rex Ryan (son of Buddy Ryan) called a timeout immediately before the play, figuring his Ravens were not in the right configuration. Brady later said he heard the whistle and that was why he stopped, but it appeared the Ravens had stopped *him*!

"Yet the referee was running toward the Patriots' side of the ball with his arms in the air to stop the play," Santos later said. "I don't know, but Brady did stop."

Then the Ravens, still ahead by 24–20, stopped Heath Evans on another fourth-down thrust, but a false-start call on the Pats' Russ Hochstein negated that play and gave the Pats one more life, sending the ball back five yards for a fourth-and-six try. That gave Brady a third chance and he pounced—scrambling 12 yards for the first down. The Ravens' Samari Rolle was nailed for illegal contact on the play and that put the ball on the 13. Brady then threw into the end zone on yet another fourth down and this time Jamaine Winborne was flagged for defensive holding. The Ravens protested, but the ball was at the eight. And then Brady hit Gaffney with the game-winner!

During this incredible climax, the Patriots weathered four offensive fourth downs—a Ravens coach calling timeout (saving Brady from being stuffed), a Patriots false start infraction negating the stop of Evans, Brady scrambling 12 yards for a first down, and then defensive holding in the end zone giving the Pats another first down before Brady hit Gaffney with the eight-yard game winner and the Ravens fell apart at the end of the game. Brady connected on only 18 of 38 throws, but still managed to pass for 257 yards and two scores with one interception.

"Brady makes the plays when they have to be made," Santos lauded. "Late in the game, if the Patriots are down by less than a touchdown, I have every faith that he'll bring them back. It's like when I covered the Celtics, late in the game if they were down by 2 or 3, if they gave the ball to Larry Bird, he'd win or tie the game. Brady is that kind of player. The thing is this: the Patriots got lucky with a couple of calls. A coach once said to me, 'It's great to be good and it's also great to be lucky once in a while.' Further, good teams win that kind of game 90 percent of the time and bad teams find ways to lose them."

Yet more almost unbelievable drama remained. The Ravens were frustrated and furious over the run of calls against them and, undoubtedly, their coordinator's timeout that wiped out their stop of Brady. The Ravens were penalized 13 times for 100 yards (to the Pats' four for 30), sending Baltimore's Bart Scott into a meltdown. After Gaffney's touchdown, he drew two 15-yard penalties for un-sportsmanlike conduct and firing an official's flag into the stands.

Still, after the kickoff, Boller unloaded a 52-yard "Hail Mary" that Mark Clayton caught at the Patriots two-yard line—before several Pats pushed him away from the goal line as time expired. "But one of the Ravens actually had Asante Samuel in a bear hug—he couldn't even move his arms," Santos noted. "I knew the game was over and was glad the pass was completed because if it was incomplete and the Patriots had been called for pass interference, the Ravens would have had a chance to either score a winning touchdown on one play or kick a field goal to send the game into overtime—because a game cannot end on a defensive penalty!"

Santos added: "The Ravens got 120 yards off two highly unusual plays. I was concerned earlier by the way Willis McGahee (138 yards off 30 carries) was running, but they got only seven yards in the fourth quarter before that last play.

Santos said he didn't see Ravens head coach Brian Billick mockingly blow three kisses to Pats' safety Rodney Harrison during an animated exchange. But he seemed pleased to hear that ex-Miami coach Don Shula, an ESPN booth guest, had backed off his claim that a Patriots' perfect season rivaling his team's unblemished 17–0 record of 35 years ago would require an asterisk. Shula was charitable to the Pats, praising them as a great team. By overcoming the Ravens, they had become only the sixth NFL team in history to go 12–0—and, more importantly, they were still in pursuit of that perfect record.

December 9, 2007 at Foxboro:
New England Patriots 34, Pittsburgh Steelers 13

Many Patriots fans considered the December 9 game at Gillette Stadium against Pittsburgh (9–3) to be the last realistic roadblock to an NFL team's first perfect *regular* season since Miami did it in 1972.

The Patriots did not need more incentive, especially after nearly losing to Baltimore, a game even Cappelletti said they should have lost. But lightly regarded Steelers safety Anthony Smith provided more incentive by actually *guaranteeing* that his team would knock off the Pats and spoil their dream of perfection! Further, former Steelers coach Bill Cowher—now a studio analyst for CBS—said his former team would win by picking on the Pats linebackers.

Brady did not pounce immediately after kickoff, but he did soon after

A View From THE BOOTH

GIL SANTOS AND GINO CAPPELLETTI 25 YEARS OF BROADCASTING THE NEW ENGLAND PATRIOTS

The WBCN Patriots' radio broadcast crew (left to right) Gil, statistician Roger Homan, producer Marc Cappello (attired in his customary sweater-vest), Gino, and engineer Dennis Knudsen

Bill Nowlin photo

A view from the booth. (left to right) Gil, Roger, Marc, and Gino.

Bill Nowlin photo

Gil's color-coded play calling sheets.

Bill Nowlin photo

Roger Homan's statistic tracking system. Every play of every Patriots game is recorded.

Bill Nowlin photo

Gino, seen here with his wife Sandy during a pre-game visit to the booth, relies on his traditional "Xs and Os" play sheets to assist him in his analysis of the games.

Bill Nowlin photo

Gino, Marc, Roger, and Gil acknowledging some fans at Gillette.

Bill Nowlin photo

Many Patriots fans can be seen at Gillette Stadium wearing Gino's replica jersey.

Bill Nowlin photo

Here are Gino and Pats QB Babe Parilli wearing the 1960s originals.

photo courtesy of Gino Cappelletti

Gino scores a TD in Fenway Park against the Bengals, December 1, 1968. It was Cincinnati's first season in the AFL. The Patriots won 33-14 before a crowd of 17,796. Note the newly introduced "sling-shot" style goalpost with the crossbar positioned directly over the goal-line. Both the AFL and NFL employed the original "H" style goalposts in the early 1960s. The goalposts were moved back to the back of the end zones, where they are now, sometime in the 1970s.

photo courtesy of Gino Cappelletti

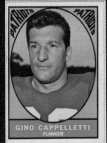

Lucy, from the "Peanuts" cartoon strip created by Charles Schulz, once declared that you could not call anyone famous unless he had his picture on a bubble gum card. By that standard Gino was quite famous during his 11-year professional football career. Here Gino is listed on one card as a kicker and on the other card he is identified as a flanker. He excelled at both, as the record books show.

Courtesy of Gino Cappelletti

During his playing days Gino also tried his hand at acting and was cast in a couple of Hollywood movies. In 1965 he was in *Never Too Late* starring Paul Ford, Connie Stevens, and Maureen O'Sullivan. In 1966 he also appeared in *Dead Heat on a Merry-Go-Round* with James Coburn (shown here).

photo courtesy of Gino Cappelletti

To: ALL RADIO PERSONNEL   From: Program Manager
cc: Leo Palmer   Date: January 11, 1971
                          Re: Gil Santos

I'm delighted to announce that Gil Santos will join the
WBZ staff February 1st.

In addition to taking over duties as "The New Voice of
the Boston Patriots", he will be doing the morning sports
show after he gets acclimated to the surroundings.

Would you please welcome Gil and make him feel at home.

Bill
Bill Shupert
BS:pr

The WBZ radio memorandum announcing Gil's assignment to the morning news team in 1971 in addition to his Patriots announcing job.

courtesy of Gil Santos

Gil may not have had his picture on a bubble gum card but he is certainly considered among the best and most famous broadcasters in the nation and is legendary in Boston. Gil is pictured here with celebrated WBZ radio broadcasters Gary LaPierre and Dave Maynard.

photo courtesy of Gil Santos

A couple of lucky young fans meet Gil and get a tour of the Patriots radio booth at Gillette Stadium.

Bill Nowlin photo

Gil and Gino will never forget the thrill of calling the Patriots' victory over St. Louis in Super Bowl XXXVI (36). Here they embrace during the post-game celebration in the Louisiana Superdome.

photo courtesy of Gil Santos

Gil holds the Super Bowl XXXVI trophy as his son Mark joins him in New Orleans after the game.

photo courtesy of Gil Santos

The two top all-time Patriot point scorers, Gino and Adam Vinatieri, share the excitement of the first NFL championship. It was a last-second Vinatieri field goal that clinched the Pats' thrilling come-from-behind victory and their first NFL championship.

photo courtesy of Gino Cappelletti

Gino and Gil lead thousands of Patriots fans on the Boston City Hall Plaza celebrating the Super Bowl XXXVI championship.

photo courtesy of Gino Cappelletti

Before most Patriots home games Patriots president Jonathan
Kraft shares his thoughts with the radio broadcast team.
He is pictured here on the Patriots sideline with WBCN field
technician Chuck Morrison while CEO Robert Kraft has a word
with wide-receivers coach Nick Caserio.

Scott Horrigan Photo

Gino interviews Head Coach Bill Belichick (seen
here in a sideline conference with quarterback Tom
Brady) before each game throughout the season.

Boston Herald photo

Howie Sylvester is WBCN's executive producer of the Patriots
Network. Here Howie cues former Patriots standout Pete Brock,
a regular contributor to the Patriots pregame show, from the
control room at the WBCN studios in Brighton.

Michael Allen photo

Pete Brock

Michael Allen photo

Randy Moss makes a crucial reception in the final game of the 2007 regular season against the New York Giants and the Patriots are the first team in history to go 16-0…

Boston Herald photo

…prompting one proud Patriots' fan, Harry Laye of Lexington, Massachusetts to commission this special edition commemorative cap.

Jim Baker photo

The number 3 played into every Patriot Super Bowl Victory and strangely does so again in their 2008 Super Bowl 17-14 loss to the New York Giants at the University of Phoenix Stadium in Glendale, Arizona (shown here). The huge numeral indicated the gate number nearest the press entrance to the facility.

Chuck Burgess photo

Normally when the Patriots are on the road the pre and post game show hosted by Gary Tanguay is broadcast from the WBCN studios in Boston. At Super Bowl XLII (42) the show was done live from the stadium radio booth. Gary and co-host Andy Gresh interview Gil and Gino shortly before kickoff. In his comments Gino warned that, although they were a superior team overall, the Patriots always had to worry about things like a crazy bounce of the ball which could change the course of any game. It turned out to be a very prophetic remark.

Chuck Burgess photo

Gil and Gino assume a pensive mood, as the events in Super Bowl XLII turn sour for the Pats. Meanwhile former Miami Dolphins coach Don Shula (back) enjoys a laugh in the radio booth next to WBCN.

Chuck Burgess photo

Meanwhile on the field Laurence Maroney runs…

Boston Herald

and Tom Brady passes his way to a go-ahead touchdown, in the final minutes of play, that seems to be the score that could win the game.

Boston Herald

Marv Albert, broadcasting from the booth adjacent to Gil and Gino, turns to his engineer with a blank expression on his face while Don Shula seems to be breathing a sigh of relief after the Giants mount their improbable scoring drive that wins Super Bowl XLII in the biggest upset imaginable.

Chuck Burgess photo

After 25 years together in the broadcast booth the relationship between the Patriots, their fans, and Gil and Gino has grown to be a very special and unique New England institution. Throughout the years, when victory has thrilled them and defeats may have caused some agony, one constant remains — their strong sense of family.

Gil is surrounded in his broadcast booth by daughter Kathy, son-in-law John, his wife Roberta, and his grandchildren Jacob and Hanna.

Photo courtesy of Gil Santos

Gino and Sandy enjoy a family vacation on Kiawah Island, South Carolina, with their family including all nine grandchildren. (Left to right) Gino, Georgia, Angela, Ella, Lea, Julia, Jack, Olivia, Brock, Emersen, Ava, and Sandy.

photo courtesy of Gino Cappelletti

the Steelers took a 3–0 edge, as a long drive led to Jeff Reed's 23-yard field goal. Brady began to work his magic and Santos was soon reporting how Brady and Moss once again were connecting regularly after relatively quiet games against Philly and Baltimore. When Brady began firing away and the star duo clicked for a four-yard touchdown and 7–3 lead late in the first quarter, Marc Cappello, resplendent once again in his good-luck sweater vest, dared to predict: "They're gonna win!"

Then Brady decided to pick on the prognosticating Steelers safety. He drew in Smith with a beautiful first-down fake handoff to Laurence Maroney and fired a picture-perfect 63-yard play-action scoring strike to wide-open Moss. Cappelletti, in a postgame interview, did not verbally jump on Smith's silly "guarantee" but said: "He's a young kid who doesn't get it yet—and I don't think the Patriots need locker-room fodder. They're above that now."

It was 14–3 and there was off-air talk in the booth of a blowout.

Then Pittsburgh stole the momentum, controlling second-period play, and rallied to 14–13 on a 32-yard Ben Roethlisberger touchdown heave to Najeh Davenport and a Jeff Reed 44-yard field goal. In response, Patriots kicker Stephen Gostkowski, who missed a previous 48-yard attempt, provided a 17–13 edge at halftime by sending one through the uprights from 42 yards.

After the halftime break, it was time for Brady to exploit the cocky Smith again.

Santos aptly labeled it "a razzle-dazzle play." Indeed, Brady flung an overhand lateral to Moss on the right side. Moss dropped it (Belichick later insisted that was not on purpose). Moss quickly scooped it up and fired a bullet pass back to Brady, who looked downfield and saw that Smith had been suckered away from coverage. Jabar Gaffney was wide open for a 56-yard score that broke open the game, 24–13.

Afterward, Brady quipped that Moss fired a better toss to him than he'd offered Moss. And it was true! Cappelletti thought Smith might have retreated in time to get a hand on Brady's bomb, but he missed "and Gaffney had good concentration to catch it." Gino also noted the Steelers had used virtually the same play in beating Seattle in the Detroit Super Bowl. "Belichick loves history and looks back to find what happened years ago, then sees if something applies now," the Duke declared. It did!

Still, Santos was verbally kicking himself because he'd said the long toss was to Donte Stallworth, not Gaffney—uniform No. 18 instead of

No. 10. "I can usually tell the difference because of Stallworth's long hair," WBCN's play-caller said. But no matter, he corrected himself and, more importantly, the Patriots were off to the races.

Brady hardly ever stopped passing—limiting rushes to only nine all game—and the Steelers never scored in the second half. Brady methodically passed the Pats downfield and with 4:35 left in the third quarter, hit Wes Welker for a two-yard TD and a 31–13 lead. Welker wound up with nine grabs, Moss and Gaffney had seven each, and Brady clicked for 399 yards and four scores. Moss stretched his NFL-leading touchdown reception total to a resounding 19!

The eventual outcome was clear, but after a tremendous goal-line stand—Pittsburgh could not score despite a third-down at the one— Welker *really* got busy. He snared four straight Brady tosses, moving Cappelletti to quip: "It's the Wes Welker show!"

Santos spoke of the Patriots advancing toward their first 99-yard drive of the season. But instead, after Moss's seventh reception, a third-down pass glanced off his hands and Gostkowski booted a 28-yard field goal with seven minutes left for the final score, 34–13. Clearly, Smith's prediction had been foolish. Clearly, Brady was unstoppable again with four scoring aerials (two to Moss) for a heaping 45, just four shy of Peyton Manning's single-season NFL record.

So the Patriots had only the woeful Jets (with that vexing memory of "Spygate"), the winless Dolphins, and a road finale with the Giants remaining in the regular season. After being defensively vulnerable for the last two games after linebacker Rosevelt Colvin was injured and lost for the season, the Patriots were stingy on defense once again—especially with that goal-line stand in a second-half shutout against the Steelers. Brady and cohorts were headed toward not only perfection but also toward NFL records galore. After two near misses plus the "blueprint" claim after the Eagles game, they were back on track in a huge way!

"It's all Belichick—he sets the pace," Cappelletti summarized about the unblemished record. "He acquired very skilled players and he brings that air of confidence. These players know they can play this game and their execution requires poise and calmness in an atmosphere filled with emotion and intensity. They operate with high efficiency—especially offensively. Belichick has that all-for-one and one-for-all philosophy and gets positive results. History will be the judge. The Super Bowl champion 49ers were built on timing and the Patriots are, too. The offensive line and those fakes prevent opponents from disrupting that timing. And it's not just Brady's arm, but his great full-body throwing motion, that gets these results."

December 16, 2007 at Foxboro:
New England Patriots 20, New York Jets 10

The soaring Patriots approached the 3–12 New York Jets' December invasion with several objectives. To keep the perfect record intact, to extract revenge for the season opener's Spygate controversy with Jets coach Eric Mangini that cost the Pats a number one draft choice and huge fines, to clinch home field advantage throughout the AFC playoffs, and to mathematically clinch the AFC championship.

Add one more element to the mix: They had to overcome atrocious weather—rain, snow, wind and bitter cold—which threatened their high-gear aerial attack. They met all but the last goal as Tom Brady failed to fire a touchdown pass for the first time all season. But Laurence Maroney, who had not been impressive in recent games, literally rushed to the rescue as a speedy workhorse, sparking a 20–10 victory with 104 yards in 26 carries plus a second-quarter score.

Santos and Cappelletti selected one other star of the game—defensive end Richard Seymour, who returned to stellar form and quickly jolted the game New England's way. On just the Jets' second play in this 97th chapter of the Pats' longest rivalry, Seymour walloped quarterback Kellen Clemens so hard that he put the starter out of commission with a rib injury, and forced a weak throw which Eugene Wilson intercepted and stepped five yards to score.

It was 7–0 within the first ten minutes of the game and the Patriots' 18th interception of 2007 had inspired thoughts of a much-desired rout of their pesky tormentors. But the weather and a decent Jets defense limited Brady, and kept the game much closer than expected. Still, Santos followed a Brady fourth-down-and-two rush for a first down at the Jet 17-yard line by observing, "He always does whatever it takes." Stephen Gostkowski's 16-yard field goal made it 10–0 at 8:51 of the second quarter.

The Jets' offense had shown nothing so far and Maroney was starting to pound away. "He's running harder today," Cappelletti suggested. But after the Pats stalled, punter Chris Hanson mishandled a snap and the Jets' David Bowens broke through to block his kick, rambling 26 yards for a touchdown. Suddenly, despite the Jets' lack of offensive punch as Mangini used three quarterbacks, the Pats lead was only 10–7.

Kelley Washington and Maroney fixed that. Washington answered Bowens' punt block with one of his own, giving the Pats possession at the Jet three, as snow-throwing fans celebrated and Maroney followed with a half-yard touchdown that returned the lead to 10 points. It was 17–7 Patriots at halftime.

All that remained amid sluggish play were a pair of fourth-quarter field goals. Mike Nugent's 33-yarder with 7:40 to play gave the Jets hope, but Gostkowski's 34-yarder with 2:52 left sealed their fate. Then it was time for the Belichick-Mangini handshake which, given the tense circumstances, went without gnashing of teeth. Belichick actually said "Good game," however unconvincingly.

So the Patriots were AFC champions with home-field advantage throughout the conference playoffs. And they became the second team to go 14–0 with Miami, which turned the trick in their perfect 1972 season, up next to close out the Foxboro portion of the regular season. "They're the second to win the first 14 games and the third to win 14 straight," Santos noted.

"The game went pretty much as I expected under the conditions," said Santos. "The Patriots had to show Maroney could run that effectively and Seymour had his best game of the season." Gino agreed, noting Maroney silenced critics by "taking a step in the right direction. The Patriots did what they needed to win. They had to put Maroney to work and he ran better with each handoff."

And what about Seymour, who had fallen off last season's form? "It was just a matter of time since he came back off a leg injury," Gino declared. "He's a magnificent player."

Cappelletti extended his analysis to the team in general. "It was not one of the Patriots' better games. It was a struggle on a bad day. They can certainly play much better, but they had pretty good control of the line of scrimmage."

Belichick stayed consistent with that one-game-at-a-time approach. But Cappelletti, with only the Dolphins (having just beaten Baltimore for their *first* win of the season) and Giants left, began talking about that perfect season. "If it doesn't happen, that would be the biggest shock," he said. Regarding the teams left to play on the Patriots schedule, and the general quality of all the teams in the NFL, Gino noted that he has been greatly impressed by the quality and play of the Patriots and Colts this season in the AFC and the Cowboys, Eagles, and Packers in the NFC. "But there are so many bad teams elsewhere in the league," he said. "I'm really noticing that now. The quality of play in the Bears-Vikings *Monday Night Football* game was an example." That contest featured two NFC Central teams and both looked like they were finding ways to lose the game (the Vikings won 20–13).

December 23, 2007 at Foxboro:
New England Patriots 28, Miami Dolphins 7

After annihilating the weak Dolphins in the season's first meeting in Miami in October, expectations were that the Patriots would slaughter them again at home in December—and in the process advance to within one victory of becoming the first NFL team to complete a regular season unbeaten and untied since Miami turned the trick in 1972.

Further, Tom Brady and Randy Moss were on record touchdown pass and reception paces for a season and the Pats were about to set a league mark for touchdowns in one season. Indeed, records were falling, but Brady and Moss would need the season climax with the Giants in New York on December 29 to set their individual marks after going scoreless in the second half of what became a 28–7 romp over the Dolphins at Gillette.

Santos and Cappelletti were incredulous as Brady and Moss hooked up for the Patriots' first two scores and a 14–0 cushion over the Dolphins, who entered the game having just avoided the specter of a winless season with an overtime triumph over Baltimore. When Brady hit Moss for an 11-yard touchdown pass in the first quarter, Cappelletti asked in disbelief, "That's a linebacker covering Moss?"

Then, after Brady capped a bullet-pass drive with a one-yard toss to Moss for a 14–0 second-quarter bulge, Tom Terrific was just two aerial scores from Peyton Manning's league mark and Moss was one shy of Jerry Rice's record. Brady had fired 47 touchdown passes and Moss had caught 21. Brady got his 48th TD pass and came within one of Manning's record with a 48-yard heave to Jabar Gaffney that created a 28–0 halftime gap and set another record—the Patriots' 71st touchdown of the season, an NFL mark.

Santos quickly pointed out that, ironically, it was the Dolphins who established the just-broken standard of 70 in 1984. "The Patriots are totally dominating this game," raved Santos, noting they'd rolled up 304 yards in one half.

Cappelletti marveled, "I'd just said that Brady threw his 47th touchdown pass and now he just fired No. 48!" Gino was impressed by

Gaffney's concentration as Miami safety Lance Schulters cut in front, leaped, and just missed the pass with a swipe before Gaffney streaked down the sideline. "It looked like an interception with Schulters flashing in front of him," Gino said.

Almost lost amid the excitement was the super running of Laurence Maroney, who had ignited the Patriots' second scoring drive with a 53-yard burst—"bang-bang" in Santos' words—and then dashed 59 untouched for the Pats' third touchdown. "He broke through like he was shot out of a cannon," yelled Santos. Gino explained that the Dolphins were so sure Brady would sneak on a third-down short-yardage play, "no one was back there after Maroney ran through. They were all in a box," he said. Maroney wound up with 156 yards on 14 carries, and eclipsed his 2006 rushing total of 745 yards on 175 runs with 789 on 166 with one game left to play in the regular season.

But as electric as Brady, Moss, and Maroney were in that lopsided first half, the Pats just flattened out afterward—Brady throwing two interceptions in their first pointless half all season. Brady also fumbled. Chris Hanson provided one highlight with a 64-yard punt, but Miami made the lone second-half score on Cleo Lemon's 21-yard scoring pass to Greg Camarillo. Santos declared: "The Patriots did not play a good third quarter and they coasted through the second half."

Still, they became the first NFL team to go 15–0 in the regular season and this was the first time they had gone undefeated in division play. They had won 18 straight regular season games, tying their own NFL mark set in 2003–04 and, with the Giants game left, had tied the NFL record for most victories in a regular season (joining the 2004 Steelers, 1998 Vikings, 1985 Bears, and 1984 49ers).

Interestingly, the Patriots, eclipsing the Dolphins' 14–0 record of 1972, also had just won game number 15 on the 25th anniversary of the infamous 1982 "Snowplow Game" against Miami at Foxboro. A work-release prison inmate named Mark Henderson, working as part of the Schaefer Stadium maintenance crew, was assigned to clear the sidelines and yard lines during the storm with a large sweeper attached to the front of a small lawn tractor. As a timeout was called just before Patriots place-kicker John Smith was about to attempt a 33-yard field goal, Henderson had just completed a clearing run across the field on the 30-yard line. Suddenly, when he approached the hash mark where Smith would be kicking from, Henderson swerved the tractor over the spot and cleared a path in the snow for Smith to cleanly approach and kick the ball. Smith made the kick, for the Patriots' incredible 3–0 victory as Dolphin coach Don Shula protested furiously.

December 29, 2007 at New York:
New England Patriots 38, New York Giants 35
The Patriots achieve a perfect regular season
and the first 16–0 regular season in NFL history

The Patriots' regular season ended where it had begun, in a rout of the Jets—at Giants Stadium. Only this time there was no "Spygate" scandal, only a fired-up Giants team that had no other motivation than to ruin dreams of the first 16–0 perfect season in NFL history.

Gil and Gino saw something of a struggle coming, but were confident that the Patriots would overcome it. Cappelletti said, "The Giants will come out and give it a good shot early, but the Patriot defense is out to win and will do so. But if the Giants get off to an early lead, that could make things interesting."

Santos predicted flat-out: "The Patriots are a better team and should win. One of the problems they're having is there's been a bullseye on their backs the last four to five weeks. The Giants will have that extra motivation, but with the defense coming around, I don't expect them to run effectively."

The NFL Network was scheduled to be the only television carrier of this historic game. But because of a populist outcry from thousands of viewers who did not subscribe to the NFL's service, or whose cable provider did not carry the NFL, political intervention ensued. Massachusetts Senator John Kerry, among others, appealed to the NFL broadcast committee to allow the game to be picked up by several networks serving the New England region. It aired on three Boston TV channels at the same time—an unprecedented occurrence, usually reserved for presidential messages like the State of the Union Address.

Because of the large number of carriers, the usual TV delay, which frustrates fans trying to listen to Gil and Gino on the radio while watching the game, varied slightly depending on the station they were watching. All of the Boston stations were in sync with each other and were delayed the same number of seconds as usual. But for some reason, the broadcast from Providence, carried on some Massachusetts cable services, had a much shorter delay—almost unnoticeable from the live radio transmission. So thousands of Pats fans watching the game at home could once again enjoy the time-honored tradition of turning down the TV and turning up the radio to hear Gil and Gino call the action.

The fans may have been comfortably settled in as they watched and listened to the game, but as things transpired, the Patriots were not. The Giants not only sprang to an early lead, but Eli Manning—younger brother of Colts' superstar Peyton Manning—exploded for four touchdown tosses. And with 9:12 gone in the third quarter, the Giants imposed the Pats' biggest deficit of the season—12 points (28–16). "The perfect season is very much in jeopardy," Santos told his WBCN audience.

It seemed the Patriots were in trouble, but this would be a night for breaking records *and* Tom Brady's usual fourth-quarter charge—this time for a 38–35 history-making victory. All three of those factors came together with 11:06 remaining in the game. Moss had uncharacteristically dropped a just-short Brady bomb on the previous play. Then with Wes Welker the intended target, but surrounded, Brady found Moss streaking down the right sideline and hit him perfectly in stride—over safety James Butler—on a 65-yard TD play that gave New England the lead for good (31–28) putting both Brady and Moss in the NFL record book via the same play. Brady had fired his 50th touchdown pass of the season, erasing Peyton Manning's league record of 49 set in 2004, and Moss had eclipsed Jerry Rice's NFL single-season touchdown reception record by one with 23. And they had clicked for a second score on this record-packed evening.

"The Patriots came right back with this after the ball he [Moss] should have caught," Cappelletti said. And Santos observed: "The Patriots have scored two unanswered touchdowns" to take the lead after the Giants were seemingly in control 28–16. The first comeback touchdown was Laurence Maroney's six-yard burst with four minutes left in chapter three, making the gap 28–23.

Yet before Brady and Moss connected in league-record fashion, they tied the Manning and Rice records on a four-yard touchdown pass, Moss out-leaping cornerback Aaron Ross for a second-quarter score. That gave the Pats a 10–7 edge and the most single-season points in league history, later ballooned to 589. "That's three records on one play," an elated Santos said. But trouble ensued.

Moss was whistled for a perfectly understandable celebration (spiking the ball) and Domenik Hixon ran the Patriots' kickoff back 74 yards for another first—the Pats allowing their first kickoff-return score of the season. And the lead suddenly was gone!

But Brady and Moss had the ultimate answer to concoct the first NFL perfect season since Miami's 1972 championship year. Lawrence Maroney followed with his second touchdown of the game, a five-yard plunge that created a 38–28 bulge. Giants star receiver Plaxico Burress, who earlier had a physical confrontation with Ellis Hobbs, closed the scoring with his second Manning connection, a three-yard toss with 1:04 remaining. It was Manning and Burress who clicked from 19 yards to give the Giants that 28–16 cushion which Brady, Moss, and Maroney had to overcome to save the perfect season.

Not to be overlooked were Wes Welker's 11 receptions for a Pats record of 122 for the season, beating Troy Brown's franchise mark, or Stephen Gostkowski's three early field goals of 37, 45, and 37 yards—the last providing a 16–14 lead before New York took a 21–16 halftime edge. Gostkowski has been a model of kicking consistency for the Patriots since the record run of Adam Vinatieri.

Referring to the comeback from another deficit, their biggest of 2007, Cappelletti concluded: "The Patriots just do what they have to do and, with those great receivers, do what champions do." Not to mention a quarterback who was AFC player of the week five times! And he just went 32 for 42 for 356 yards and two touchdown strikes to his favorite target, Randy Moss!

The veteran announcer and analyst had a funny exchange with 1:01 left and Brady in kneel-down mode, killing the clock. "It's the first time an NFL team has gone 16–0," Santos declared. Cappelletti answered, "I think you can say that now." And Santos said as both laughed, "I always like to be cautious."

At the conclusion of the broadcast the usually very expressive Santos in a rare moment where he seemed to have to search for his words simply said to his audience, "What a season, what a season! It has been a privilege to call this team." Gino, in his usual understated fashion, concurred by the mere word "Ditto."

Sixteen wins and no losses—a new regular-season NFL record. Gil and Gino had called the perfect season. What more could they say?

12

THE PLAYOFFS

"I just marvel at their longevity. They know each other so well and they're so excellent together, their broadcasts are almost seamless. Their whole low-key approach gives you a solid, steady call of the game. You don't hear flash and dash—just a solid call of the game. Gil has been amazingly helpful to me with his approach to a game."—**DAVE GOUCHER**, BRUINS PLAY-BY-PLAY VOICE ON WBZ RADIO

2008 AFC EAST DIVISIONAL CHAMPIONSHIP

January 12, 2008 at Foxboro:
New England Patriots 31, Jacksonville Jaguars 20

Now it was playoff time and the postseason tournament of the NFL was upon them. With each victory, you moved ahead. One loss and your season was over. The challenge to the Patriots was to win their next three games and do what no other team in NFL history had ever done.

By virtue of their best win-loss record in their conference (or in the world at that time!), the undefeated Patriots had clinched a bye in the first round and home-field advantage throughout the playoffs. The team was able to get some well-deserved rest as the wild-card round began.

On Saturday, January 5, 2008 the Seahawks were victorious over the Redskins, earning the right to travel to Green Bay to challenge the Packers. That same day, the Jaguars fought their way to their meeting in Foxboro by beating Pittsburgh 31–29. On Sunday of that same weekend, the New York Giants beat the Buccaneers 24–14 and the Chargers of San Diego advanced, defeating the Tennessee Titans, 17–6.

Tonight's game in New England was the second Divisional game of the weekend. Earlier in the day, the Packers dominated the Seattle Seahawks in snowy Green Bay, 42–20. Now the nation turned its attention to New England for the 8:15 kickoff, televised on CBS with Jim Nance and Phil Simms reporting from the booth next to Gil, Gino, and the WBCN radio crew.

It was a beautiful Saturday night for football in Foxboro, with temperatures in the high 30s with little or no wind—a relatively balmy evening in the Northeast. The tailgaters that were spread around Gillette Stadium for miles north and south created an atmosphere reminiscent of what a Civil War encampment must have been like. Open fires dotting the outlying landscape, the smell of cooking meat, and raucous talk about the upcoming confrontation. Drawing closer to this battlefield, however, the analogy grew less apt as gas-driven generators provided the power to run wide-screen plasma televisions perched inside of luxuriously appointed tents and recreational vehicles fit for a sultan and his harem. Gas grills loaded with steaks, ribs, sausages, shrimp, and even a boiling lobster or two were everywhere. Adult beverages ranged from beer and wine to frozen concoctions prepared with portable blenders on makeshift bars worthy of the finest restaurant or pub. In short, it was an amazing atmosphere full of anticipation, excitement, and high expectations for the thousands of fans lucky enough to be able to attend the game.

The Patriots' opening playoff test, with Jacksonville, for the AFC Divisional Championship will be remembered as tense and tried for a half, but will also be remembered for Tom Brady setting yet another NFL passing record as the perfect-record Pats seized control—and for Gil Santos making a marvelous analogy on Brady's most colorful completion.

Gino opened the broadcast by commenting to Gil about the excitement outside the booth, which was palpable by game time. "The excitement is something else when you are in the playoffs. The players will tell you that it's just another game, and it is, but the intensity is stepped up a notch. The best of the best are here, yet it comes back to playing football, playing well and executing the way you are capable of."

The beginning of the game was like a tennis match—back and forth, back and forth. Each time one team had the ball, it would drive down the field and score. Each drive consumed so much time that the first half seemed to fly by. With about four minutes left in the second period, Gino turned to Gil and Roger off the air and remarked with astonishment, "I can't believe this game is moving so fast. There have only been three possessions by the Patriots and three for the Jags so far and it's almost halftime. Amazing."

At the two-minute warning with the score tied at 14, the Pats had the ball on the Jacksonville 19 yard line and a first down. It looked like a sure thing for them to drive it in for the final score of the half and go into the locker room with a seven-point lead, 21–14. But on the next play, the Pats drew a 15-yard penalty for an illegal block that in turn led to a 33-yard field goal attempt with the clock running out of time. The kick was no good and the score remained tied. Gil Santos' final words of the half were, "We have seen quite a game so far. I wonder what the second half will bring. The Pats will get the ball when they return."

The Pats broke from the 14–14 intermission deadlock to forge ahead of their stubborn foes on Brady's second and third touchdown tosses, leading 28–20. Tom Terrific, never more accurate, then spotted Donte Stallworth streaking down the right sideline. What followed was a perfect connection.

Brady let fly a tremendous 53-yard aerial that Stallworth accepted in full stride at the Jaguar 26. Santos described the play with precision. "It was a marvelous throw," he said with excitement resonating, "and Stallworth made a catch like Willie Mays in the 1954 World Series."

Indeed he did, and the comparison with perhaps the best catch in baseball history was absolutely striking! It's precisely this kind of quick, colorful, and dramatic observation that separates Santos from other Boston-area sports play-callers. He is one of a deeply talented veteran breed that included Ned Martin, Curt Gowdy, Jon Miller, Ken Coleman, Johnny Most, Bob Wilson, and John Carlson.

If you have ever witnessed a Patriots game in the stadium and listened to the broadcast of the game by Gil and Gino, you will appreciate what Bill Braken, a WBCN engineer who has worked with the announcing duo for years, observed. "You can be watching the game or see a play unfold before your eyes, you are thinking about what you are seeing, but Gil's description of what is going on is better than what you can see yourself. He sees things you don't even see, tells you about them and you go, 'Oh yeah that's right, that's good, that's what I am seeing'—it's incredible. And right after that Gino has something to say that helps you understand something that went on during the play that you might not have even been aware of. It makes for a fantastic experience." Gil has often remarked about great athletes like Randy Moss, Larry Bird, or Ted Williams making something so hard to do look so easy and effortless when they do it; that certainly applies to him as well. Gil makes something so very difficult—expertly calling the often-frenetic action of a

Patriots game—sound so natural and easy. Add the astute observations of Cappelletti and you have a classic combination for the ages.

After Brady and Stallworth clicked again for nine yards, Stephen Gostkowski connected with a field goal from 35 yards, atoning for a miss of that length, to seal a 31–20 victory loaded with aerial highlights.

Brady's latest league mark was connecting on 92 percent of his passes, 26 of 28—best ever in the NFL postseason—and he did so with usual star receiver Randy Moss catching only one pass, a key early fourth-down pitch of 14 yards. Brady, never sacked, would have been perfect if not for Wes Welker and Benjamin Watson dropping well-thrown tosses. Yet Welker did catch nine and Watson snared a pair of six-point heaves.

Santos conceded, "The Jaguars took Moss out of the game (by double-teaming him), but Brady spread things around to his wealth of receivers." Beyond Welker's nine receptions, Kevin Faulk had five, Stallworth and Jabar Gaffney three each in a spectacular show. Watson caught two for touchdowns and Laurence Maroney, who also caught a pair, was outstanding with 122 yards and a TD, off 22 carries.

As cohesive as the Patriots offensive stars were, so were Santos and Cappelletti in one of their best games together. And they were very fair to the wild-card visitors who had Foxboro fans nervous throughout the first half. "The Patriots met a stern test tonight," said Gino. "Jacksonville gave the Patriots the good fight. I was very impressed with the Jaguars."

It was not clear for some time that the Pats would roll to 17–0, not with the Jaguars offering an imposing two-back rushing attack and unsung quarterback David Garrard passing surprisingly well, alternating handoffs and heaves to Fred Taylor and Maurice Jones-Drew. They moved smartly from the opening kickoff, driving 80 yards to score as Garrard hit Mercedes Lewis for 34 yards and, with Mike Vrabel nearly sacking him, finding Matt Jones for a six-yard score.

But Brady responded later in the first quarter, hitting Maroney for 33 yards, Moss for 14 on fourth down (Moss's lone catch) and spotting Watson in the back of the end zone for a three-yard tying touchdown. "Brady gets credit because he put the ball in the only spot where it could be caught," Cappelletti analyzed. "And Watson made a great catch."

Then Ty Warren, playing an aggressive game, whacked Garrard, forcing a fumble that Vrabel recovered at the Jaguar 29. Faulk spun nine yards with a pass and Maroney tripped nine yards to the one before scoring on the second quarter's initial play. The Pats led, 14–7, but Garrard was ready with another long drive. This one went 95 yards in 7:46 and Garrard created a halftime deadlock with a six-yard TD strike to Ernest Wilford.

The Pats were stunned because Garrard kept coming back, leading sustained drives with his talented, if under-rated, cohorts and wound up solidly completing 22 of 33 passes for 278 yards and two touchdowns. But Jones-Drew and Taylor were limited to a combined 66 yards on 19 thrusts.

By contrast, Maroney enjoyed the first 100-yard playoff game of his career, gaining 122 yards off 22 carries, with that second-quarter touchdown, and two catches for 40 yards.

It was Brady's penchant for the dramatic that really turned this game. After Maroney scampered 22 yards and Brady hit Gaffney for 13 to the six, the quarterback turned into an incredible actor. On a fake direct snap to Faulk, Brady hid the ball, leaped, and turned his back to hide the ball in his right hand while thrusting his left arm high in the air reminiscent of the classic "Statue of Liberty" play, for tremendous effect. The entire front line of Jacksonville fell for Brady's fake, as he fired a delayed strike to Welker for the six-yard score that broke the tie with 8:49 to play in the third quarter. Brady could have gotten an Oscar for his acting!

Josh Scobee interrupted the Pats' attempt to extend the lead with his first of two field goals, a 39-yard hit that cut the Pats' advantage to 21–17. But going for three points against the unblemished Pats is a type of surrender. And the Patriots took advantage of the Jags' willingness to settle when Brady found Watson for his second score, a nine-yard reception that carried the team into the fourth quarter with a 28–17 bulge.

That was Brady's third touchdown pass of the night and 53rd of the extended season. "Brady found Watson perfectly, over the middle in between two defenders," Cappelletti said. After Scobee connected from 25 yards to make it 28–20, Gostkowski answered from 35 for the 11 point final spread. "This time it's perfect," said Santos, alluding to Gostkowski's first-half wide-right miss that he had figured was "big."

There was one more league record set that night. Rodney Harrison punctuated the triumph with an interception, tying an NFL mark by doing so in four straight playoff games. That was one of only two Garrard mistakes, but Brady didn't make any. He completed his first 16 heaves, then saw Watson mishandle one in the third period. Wes Welker also had a potentially costly drop in the final stanza. But Brady had all the other answers—along with that remarkable receiver corps and Maroney.

"Jacksonville turned the ball over twice, but the Patriots turned it over not at all," Santos summarized. That was a huge difference in a tight drama. And the bomb to Stallworth was an ideal exclamation. "It was a terrific play," said Santos. "Donte just flung himself forward with a great individual effort," agreed Gino.

The Patriots had just won the AFC Eastern Division Championship Game and would have to wait until the next day to find out who they would face—again in the friendly confines of Gillette Stadium—for the American Football Conference title and a trip to the Super Bowl.

All eyes would be on the Sunday afternoon contest at the RCA Dome in Indianapolis where the Chargers faced the favored Colts. The standard line from all of the Patriots players and coaches in the locker room was that they had no preference as to whom they would face—a mantra that was recited throughout the playoffs—because the best team will be the one that wins.

In a seesaw battle, the Chargers outlasted and stunned the defending Super Bowl champions, 28–24. The game came down to the wire but every Patriots fan in New England knew before the game was even into the last quarter that the Colts would lose. The reason? The Colts fans committed an unpardonable sin at the end of the third quarter that New England fans knew would anger the Football Gods.

During the break between the third and fourth quarters of the Colts—Chargers divisional playoff game broadcast on CBS television with Dan Dierdorf and Greg Gumbel as hosts, the on-field introduction of the national NFL Punt, Pass and Kick contest finalists were televised across the network. The annual event, open to boys and girls from eight to 15 years of age, had started earlier in the fall with local, then regional, and finally national competitions. It was an extraordinary accomplishment for the boys and girls who made it to the national level.

Each age group champion was introduced to the stadium and national television audience with each contestant wearing a jersey representing the NFL team closest to where they lived. In the 14- to 15-year-old division, the champion was Anna Grant from Stratham, New Hampshire and of course she wore the team jersey of the New England Patriots.

In a display of incredibly boorish behavior, the Colts fans roundly and loudly booed, jeered, and tried to humiliate the young lady. In a display of her New England breeding, she courageously laughed off the low-brow behavior of the partisan Indianapolis crowd. Sure enough, the Colts lost and young Anna became the center of attention, honored by the Kraft family when she was invited to take part in the opening coin-toss at the AFC championship game in Foxboro the following Sunday.

2008 AFC CHAMPIONSHIP GAME

January 20 at Foxboro:
New England Patriots 21, San Diego Chargers 12

The evening before the big game in Foxboro, reporters, and assorted members of the press were collecting their credentials for the AFC championship inside the media workroom next to the Patriot locker room and beneath the northwest, or open end of Gillette Stadium—the end where the stylized lighthouse is located. One member of the gathered media wandered out alone and on to the playing field of the cavernous stadium. The bright lights were on and seemed particularly intense as they shone on the pristine green turf and empty blue and red plastic seats. Just a few workers were visible from the field, hanging some new advertising banners and making other preparations for the game. Upon reflection, the reporter observed that it reminded him of the famous scene in the 1976 movie *Rocky* when Rocky Balboa paid a late-night visit to the empty arena—the Philadelphia Spectrum—where he would fight for the championship the next day. There was *something* in the air that night, and *something* in the air *this* night in Foxboro. Though indefinable, it hinted of exciting and extraordinary events to come.

Preparations had been going on all week for the big game. At the Town Square Diner in nearby Norwood, the breakfast special Sunday morning was "Patriot Pancakes," a delicious red, white, and blue culinary creation of blueberry pancakes smothered in fresh ripe strawberries topped with a dollop of rich whipped cream. Down the road at the Staples store on the Providence Highway, a half dozen San Diego fans, all dressed in powder blue and yellow replica Chargers jerseys, were buying poster boards and markers to create some visible support for their team. In some good-natured but passionate exchanges with local Pats fans, the San Diego supporters predictably made the absurd comment that the only reason the Patriots could win and had won so many games was by cheating. "You guys had to take illegal videos in New York in order to win—you're cheaters!" Yady yady ya...To which one of the Pats' fans simply replied, "Hey what about when we crushed you guys 38 to 14 earlier this season, we didn't need anything but our pure talent to win that one!" Unmoved, the Chargers fans continued their trash talk and gleefully headed out to their vehicles for the short ride south to Foxboro.

Even though the game was scheduled for a 1 p.m. start and the sun was brilliantly shining, the playing conditions this week stood in marked contrast to the previous game. A cold front had swept across the east and down from Canada. It brought with it temperatures that would not rise above 20 degrees and a brisk northwesterly wind that made the windchill temperature near eight degrees above zero. It was cold. It was frostbite weather.

The cold temperatures hardly put a damper on the enthusiasm of Pats fans at their tailgate parties and in the seats of the stadium during the game. Resourceful New Englanders erected a makeshift tent and shelter city around Gillette. Propane heaters joined the usual compliment of campfires and generator powered electrical heaters in every nook and cranny imaginable that provided shelter from the elements. Inside the park, all manner of cold weather clothing—some fashionable, some pretty bizarre—was seen. Despite the frigid conditions, a sea of red, white, and blue Patriots apparel found its way to the top layers of many a fan's wardrobe. The fans were ready for this one.

Gil Santos and Gino Cappelletti were also ready for this one, very ready, not only in their broadcast preparations but also in their cold weather clothing preparations. Gino, always fashionable (the Duke), retained his usual suede overcoat but wisely layered sweaters and thermals underneath. Gil—the guy who loves to experience the game from the booth as closely as possible to the way the fans experience it in the stands—probably was better prepared for the below-freezing weather than anyone in ballpark. He had on the puffiest hooded down jacket you could ever imagine—he looked like an arctic explorer on a Discovery Channel documentary. His puffy black nylon parka made the Michelin Man look anorexic. He was all set for whatever Mother Nature threw his way.

As the well-insulated announcers made their way through the fans in the main concourse to the broadcast booth at midfield, they were greeted, as they have been for the last three seasons, by friendly Scott Augustine, the Gillette events staff security person assigned to monitor access to the area. Scott, wearing his hard to miss florescent orange

"Team Operations" jacket, was at his usual post at the press box entry door. Tall and thin, his bearded face was barely visible behind a snugged-up hooded sweatshirt and his bright orange baseball cap. Greeting the personable announcers at every home game is a ritual that Scott enjoys tremendously. "Gil and Gino are the nicest guys you could ever imagine. They are always so nice and polite to me and I see that they are the same way with all of the people who come up to them when they walk in to the press box."

The duo entered the WBCN radio booth to find it a lot more active that usual. It would remain so throughout the game. Besides the usual complement of engineers and technical staff, Gary Tanguay and Andy Gresh elected to remain in the booth for this game to take their game notes and prepare for their postgame show. Marc Katic, a reporter and news anchor for WBZ radio, was also on hand as he prepared his special report about this big game. To add to the mix, many of the advertisers and sponsors of the broadcast had the opportunity to stop by the booth, spending a little time there throughout the game, escorted in and out diplomatically by Chris Rucker, the station's promotions manager.

Despite the hubbub all around them, once Gil and Gino settled into their familiar stations and focused on the field, it was all business. Someone could have brought in a disco ball and the Solid Gold Dancers and it would not have mattered one whit to the announcers. That is how focused they became covering this AFC Championship game.

As the singing of the National Anthem was nearing the end, the crowd in Gillette began the usual anticipatory ovation by cheering and clapping. This time the fans were energized even more than usual by a well-coordinated fly-over by a squad of F-16 jets piloted by the Vermont Air National Guard.

In a game of apparent psychological warfare, the Chargers delayed their entry into the stadium. Instead of coming out of the locker room tunnel onto the field when the public address announcer introduced them, they huddled in the tunnel and made their way out rather haphazardly as the Patriots were being greeted by the fans. Maybe the southern Californians were just really cold and wanted to stay out of the wind as long as possible. In any event, the best moment of the pregame ceremonies was when young Anna Grant, the Punt, Pass, and Kick champion who was booed in Indianapolis, was brought out on to the field for the coin toss and received a rousing cheer from the New England fans.

*

Through most of this incredible season, the perfect-record Patriots depended on league MVP Tom Brady and his sensational corps of receivers to prevail over foes with record-setting efforts. But the AFC title game against injury-riddled San Diego brought distinct changes.

For one thing, Brady—who fired an NFL-record 50 touchdown passes in leading the Pats to the NFL's first 16–0 regular season and three more in dispatching Jacksonville in the playoff opener—had lost much of his brilliance. He was intercepted three times by the defensively tough Chargers.

But the big story was how 5'8", 202-pound Laurence Maroney, who had rolled up 122 yards and a touchdown for the second straight game, took over for the inconsistent Brady in the second half with a power-running attack that produced 106 of his yards. His co-star was Kevin Faulk, who made a spectacular diving first-down catch, among his eight receptions for 87 yards.

Also played down for much of the season was the nevertheless solid defense, that in this title tilt kept the Chargers out of the end zone. One sensational play belonged to Junior Seau, when he kept the Patriots ahead by crashing through the line on third down and nailing Michael Turner for a two-yard loss at the Pats' six. That forced a fourth field goal by Nate Kaeding—this one from 24 yards. That is all San Diego had to show for its cross-country trip to frigid Foxboro—field goals!

"Seau shot the gap!" Santos exclaimed, realizing he had just called a game-turning play against Seau's ex-team and hometown team—even though 8:31 remained in the third chapter. Santos noted the Chargers twice had first downs at the Patriot nine and wound up with just three points each time.

Cappelletti joined in: "If one of those field goals had been a touchdown, it might have been a different game. But the Patriot defense shut it down, though the Chargers fought the good fight."

When San Diego still had a faint vision of a comeback and Faulk made that diving catch on third-and-11, rolling two yards to a first down and realistically dashing all Charger hopes, "What a GREAT player this kid is!" Santos yelled about the usual role player. Then Faulk hauled in another short pass for a first down on the next series, adding emphasis to what Gil had just said.

But San Diego coach Norv Turner, who had seen his team stun the

Colts in Indianapolis a week earlier and had his team hit Foxboro with an eight-game victory skein, said Asante Samuel's second-quarter interception of hobbled Philip Rivers was the big play. The Pats' lead was only 7–6 at the time and Samuel reached in to pry the ball away from Chris Champers at the Chargers 24.

"Samuel ripped it right away from him," Gino declared. "Rivers was going down and should not have thrown the pass." Samuel returned the ball to the San Diego 24 and just two plays later, Brady found Jabar Gaffney with his first of two TD strikes, a 12-yarder. "Gaffney caught it and exploded," Gino described after Stephen Gostkowski's PAT gave the Patriots a little breathing room at 14–6.

But the stubborn Chargers stayed close and intercepted Brady for a third time.

Brady, now the fastest NFL quarterback to reach 100 victories in a career, tossed a screen pass to Wes Welker that gained 10 yards. Maroney cutbacks sent him 20 yards to the Chargers 20. Then Brady's screen to Maroney netted 11 and the second-year running back followed with a dash to the six and a first-down thrust to the one. The Chargers may have been looking for Maroney again, but Brady found Welker, who fell into the end zone with 12:15 left.

Brady's third interception had been especially galling. Maroney, again the big story, ran the ball smartly and Randy Moss caught an 18-yard pass. Moss had only one reception for the second straight playoff game, but his ominous presence helped the other receivers get free. And Moss did have a colorful 14-yard end-around pickup. But another Brady interception by a leaping Antonio Cromartie came in the end zone, returned to the two, after Brady and Maroney seemed to have the Pats en route to a big score.

"Tom did not see Cromartie at all," said Cappelletti. And after the Patriots held the Chargers deep in their own end after what appeared to be a costly turnover, Santos said simply: "The defense came up big!" Indeed it did and the Maroney Express was off toward the clinching touchdown, which Maroney set up, and Welker scored on the short pitch from Brady, who wound up with 22 completions of 33 aerials for 209 yards and two touchdowns, but with three uncharacteristic pickoffs.

San Diego was at a disadvantage with Rivers hobbling on a bad knee, unable to throw with much force but still directing his team well. Talented tight end Antonio Gates was also playing hurt and LaDainian Tomlinson, the NFL's top rusher, was unable to try more than two early runs. But Michael Turner was strong in his place, amassing 65 yards in 17 attempts.

Rivers seemed so iffy that CBS analyst Bill Cowher, the former Pittsburgh coach, pitched at halftime for Chargers coach Turner to replace him. Turner would have none of that and Rivers completed 19 of 37 for 211 yards. But he had no touchdowns and threw two interceptions. "Still, it was a gutsy performance on a banged-up knee," Cappelletti said.

As the clock began to wind down in the fourth period, great ball control by the Brady offense began to gradually relax the tension of fans and the crew in the press box. As Gil Santos called the final action, his voice over the air remained calm but his body language in the booth was anything but. "Brady to Welker... to the San Diego 40... Maroney to the 19 on an incredible open field run!" (Santos executes a fist pump high in the air over his head.) "Screen pass to Laurence Maroney to the 11 yard line... a six-yard touchdown toss to Wes Welker!" (Gil does a double fist pump this time) "With 12:15 left in the final period the Patriots really came up big when they had to!"

The 21–12 score stood as Brady and company played ball control during the last nine minutes, forcing San Diego to use all of its timeouts early. Just before the two-minute warning, Gino exclaimed that, "The Patriots are now just two minutes and 11 seconds away from going to their fourth Super Bowl in seven years!" Truly a magnificent achievement.

A phalanx of Massachusetts State Police gathered in the visiting team tunnel while a sea of orange-jacketed stadium security guards formed ranks in the open end of the field in anticipation of the final seconds of the game and a victory for the home team.

The crowd seated below the WBCN booth turned and with arms raised in celebration began to chant, "Gil, Gil, Gil, Gil!" then "Gi-no, Gi-no, Gi-no!" After getting the expected wave of acknowledgement from the radio booth, the happy revelers turned the attention to the TV booth and began, "Jim. Jim, Jim (Nantz)!" And "Phil, Phil, Phil (Simms)!"

The fans got the desired response and turned happily to the field where Tom Brady took a knee on the last two plays and as the victory became inevitable, Gil Santos said, "This one was a tough one to win but boy oh boy what a game! The Pats are 18 and 0... they have beaten the San Diego Chargers 21 to 12!"

As the final gun sounded, several large cannons on the sideline exploded and sent tons of red, white, blue, and silver confetti high into the air. Whipped and supported by the gusting wind, the sparkling paper lingered in the air as a portable stage was rolled onto the field and the presentation ceremony for the AFC championship trophy was conducted.

Although this was nowhere near the 38–14 pounding that the Patriots laid on San Diego back on September 16 (one game after the Spygate controversy and just after Tomlinson and other Chargers, badly stung by the Pats' 24–21 year-earlier postseason upset in San Diego, had shot off their mouths about Bill Belichick) it was a great victory. The 21–12 win was a tribute to the team play of the Patriots—one part of their game rising to the occasion when another was faltering. This time it was the big plays of the defense. As Gino Cappelletti noted, "All the San Diego scoring was on field goals. The Patriot defense came up big when it had to, stopping the Chargers in the red zone time after time. The Patriots crossed up the San Diego offense by mixing up their looks and playing really tough. Their goal now is not just the best record for a season, but for all time." he exclaimed as down on the field owner Bob Kraft grasped the Lamar Hunt Trophy just won by the AFC champion Patriots.

The moment Gil and Gino signed off the air, they turned and exchanged heartfelt hugs and high fives with Marc, Roger, the entire technical crew, and with each other. It was the final broadcast of the season—a perfect season—from Foxboro. The significance of what they had experienced and witnessed this year was clearly understood and appreciated by everyone—if not in words, then in their private celebration.

Producer Mark Cappello could spare little time enjoying the moment. He quickly packed up the mobile equipment he needed to send the locker room interviews of the players back to Gary Tanguay and his cohorts hosting the WBCN postgame show. As Marc hurried from the press box, through the concourse to the media elevator that would shuttle him beneath the stands to the locker room, he could not help but notice a very beautiful sight.

The sky above Foxboro had turned inky black, not a cloud was evident, as the waxing full moon had risen with unusual brightness above the closed end of the stadium. In front of nature's light show, thousands upon thousands of confetti shards still hung in the air reflecting the moonlight and the lights of the stadium as they slowly covered the field and the thousands of fans below who refused to leave until every moment of this night was taken in.

Hundreds of media people gathered in a holding area under the main concourse waiting to be allowed into the locker room for interviews or to attend the team press conference in the adjacent auditorium. After about 10 or 15 minutes, the doors to the locker room opened and Robert Kraft walked out leading a line of Patriots brass, friends, and family members. He was holding the Hunt Trophy proudly before him as he stopped to say a few words to the Fox Television reporters. When he was finished, the members of the press were allowed in to speak with the players.

You might expect that on a day (now evening) like this, there would be a joyous celebration in the locker room. A celebration, for example, like the one witnessed in the Red Sox locker room when they clinched the American League Championship at Fenway Park back in October.

What went on behind closed doors before the media went into the room is anyone's guess. But there was no evidence of popped champagne, no plastic sheeting to protect the walls and lockers, no eye goggles, no Irish step dancing to the music of the Dropkick Murphys— nothing like that at all.

Instead, the players who greeted the press were all quite happy but calm and collected. A few were wearing their brand new AFC Champion caps, but other than that, it seemed no different than the scene after any other good win at home. Reporters and camera operators swarmed "like ants to some goodies at a picnic," according to Cappello— toward each new player who entered the room or emerged from a shower. Whether it was Matt Light, Heath Evans, Laurence Maroney, Kyle Brady, Tedy Bruschi, Junior Seau, or rookie Brandon Meriweather, they all received the press with courtesy and a common response.

They had one more game to play.

After the press conferences and interviews were finished, the Patriots quietly went off to watch the NFC Championship game to see just *who* that last game would be against. If it was cold in Foxboro, it was even colder in Green Bay, where the Giants upset the Packers in a thriller, 23–20.

The Patriots were instantly heavily favored to repeat what they did to realize a perfect regular season—beat the New York Giants. Only this time it would be to cap the best NFL season ever.

13

A ONE-GAME SEASON

"Nobody in sports broadcastings paints a better word picture than Gil Santos, and Gino explains things so well in that comfortable, folksy way of his. They both tell it like it is no matter what."—**JOE CASTIGLONE**, RADIO VOICE OF THE 2007 WORLD CHAMPION BOSTON RED SOX

SUPER BOWL XLII

February 3, 2008 at Glendale, Arizona:
New York Giants 17, New England Patriots 14

THE HYPE began very early this time.

For 42 years the NFL Championship game, popularly called the *Super Bowl* since 1967, has been a sporting event like no other on earth. Ever since "Broadway Joe" Namath boldly predicted that his New York Jets team from the upstart American Football League would win Super Bowl III in 1969 (which they did), the NFL Championship game has become the biggest media extravaganza in America, if not the world.

The National Football League estimated that when the Patriots were in Super Bowl XXXIX (39), on February 6, 2005, 143,600,000 people watched at least a portion of the game on television. Clearly this football game has become something very special.

When Broadway Joe made his promise the 1969 TV audience only numbered 55 million viewers, a fraction of today's audience. But the game certainly captured the attention of the American public as Namath made good on his prediction. The New York Jets shocked the Colts 27–23 for the first AFL Super Bowl victory, which was instrumental in both the eventual merger of the leagues and the escalation of the annual war of words that has preceded every Super Bowl since.

Some tabloid material surfaced in the days following the Patriots' AFC title triumph over San Diego when Tom Brady, who played in 126 straight games, was seen in New York wearing a walking boot on his right foot. He was with supermodel girlfriend Gisele Bundchen and was fa-voring his right foot as he walked with her. Brady had also appeared to limp from his news conference Sunday after the Patriots' 21–12 win over the Chargers. But he made little of it, assuring questioners that he would not miss the Super Bowl against the New York Giants.

The question of Brady's ailing ankle was seemingly put to rest on a cold Sunday morning in Foxboro when he appeared to walk without dis-comfort as he made a brief appearance before thousands of screaming fans and a slew of television cameras at the Super Bowl send-off rally held at Gillette Stadium.

"Rally Sunday" took place on January 27, 2008 and Patriots fans were five or six abreast in a line a half-mile long outside of Gillette Stadium at eight o'clock in the morning for the 11 a.m. event. A light, fluffy snow-fall began to coat the fans as they waited patently to enter the stadium to send their heroes off to the Super Bowl in grand fashion. The tem-perature was 27 degrees.

At 8:30 the Patriots' stadium security mercifully opened the gates and the fans rushed inside to stake claim to the nearest seats to the field they could get. At midfield about 20 yards back from the stands, a portable stage decorated with red, white, and blue bunting was in place. It was the same platform the Patriots had rolled out to accept their AFC cham-pionship trophy after the Jacksonville game two weeks before.

As the intensity and nature of the snowfall changed into to a hard-driving sleet and snow mix, the fans continued to fill up the lower bowl of Gillette. The official estimate of fans who braved the weather to cheer on their team was at least 16,000. The sizable Sunday morning turnout prompted Stacey James, the Pats media liaison to comment, "This is amazing. I can recall when we didn't have this many fans in the old sta-dium for a *game!*"

As Gil and Gino arrived at 9 a.m., they checked their suitcases for the trip to Arizona with the staff from the Paul Arpin Van Lines company. All of the gear would be trucked to the airport, Logan this time, and be loaded aboard the giant Boeing 767 that would take them and the team to Phoenix. After the rally, all of the players, coaches, support staff, and media would be screened by the TSA at Gillette and then would convoy into Boston on six giant motor coaches.

Out on the field, a platoon of colonial-attired patriot re-enactors with smoking muskets, the Patriots cheerleaders, and team mascot Pat Patriot were entertaining the large crowd. Dan Roche of WBZ TV and former Patriots quarterback Scott Zolak were on stage as the opening act.

By 10:30 it was time for Gil and Gino to make their way to the field. Dan Roche introduced Gil as the emcee for the remainder of the rally and for the introduction of the players and coaches. The boisterous, snow-covered crowd acknowledged the introduction by chanting "Gil, Gil, Gil, Gil!" over and over again. The first person Gil introduced and welcomed onto the stage with him was his partner. Again, the happy fans began a new chant, "Gi-no, Gi-no, Gi-no!" as the former Patriots star jogged smartly across the field and up to the platform. The excitement continued to build as more video of the Patriots' unprecedented 18-game undefeated run to the Super Bowl was shown on the big stadium screens in each end zone. Of course the dramatic and stirring musical soundtrack of the video was accompanied by narration taken directly from the radio broadcasts of Gil and Gino.

Massachusetts Governor Deval Patrick addressed the crowd to a mix of cheers and jeers. This was not a political event and he good-naturedly recognized that fact while offering the congratulations of the Common-wealth to the team, coaches, and to owner Robert Kraft.

Wild cheers greeted the team and coaches as they were finally introduced. Junior Seau, dapper in a hip "pork pie" hat delighted the fans as he led them in some impromptu cheers and chants. The biggest cheers of the day were reserved for Bill Belichick and Tom Brady. Quickly the team was ushered off the field, out of the driving snowfall, and into the stadium to make their way to the TSA screening and the buses that would take them to the airport.

The week preceding Super Bowl XLII was no exception to the annual frenzy that has become known as Super Bowl Week. In fact, the annual "media day" early in the week—where the players and coaches of both the Patriots and Giants met and had to respond to thousands of press inquiries—was more like a media *circus*. The National Football League issued a whopping 4,786 media credentials. The officially credentialed reporters included one woman dressed in a wedding gown—she asked Tom Brady to marry her.

For every dozen legitimate members of the press asking intelligent football questions, there seemed to be one with a pet monkey or a hand puppet asking the most ridiculous questions imaginable. Perhaps it served as comic relief for the teams, lessening a bit of the pressure that would come with the final preparations for the game to come.

In the eyes of partisan Patriots fans the legitimate national media continued to raise bogus issues and stir controversy throughout the week—almost anything to try to taint the incredible accomplishments of the Patriots and Tom Brady. Rehashing any and all things that were distractions to the team during a season full of them, the media replays became distractions in themselves. Even well-meaning Boston Mayor Tom Menino unintentionally added still another "incident" with his premature announcement of a Patriots victory parade and rally after the Super Bowl. Besides being perfect locker room bulletin board material to charge up the Giants, Menino incurred the wrath of Patriots Nation, fearful that his leaked plan would jinx the team. Of course making preparations for the *probability* of victory parade was something that had to be done. Even the city officials in New York were *quietly* planning for the *possibility* of a parade for the Giants. It was the public announcement of the Boston plan that caused consternation. On top of all that, the prematurely announced celebration was going to conflict with the Massachusetts primary election day! Both the Boston City Hall rally location and the Copley Square parade launching spot would prevent thousands of voters from getting to their polling places. Super Bowl Parade vs. Super Tuesday primary. What a mess it would be if that happened!

Expectations were high that the Patriots would win—convincingly—over the Giants. Almost everyone, even some of the same critics who had bashed the Pats during the season, was on board. Many pundits were genuinely convinced and had been for a long time, that the Patriots were possibly the best NFL team ever to take the field and that this game would prove that to be true.

Troy Aikman, who quarterbacked the Dallas Cowboys to three Super Bowl triumphs, was effusive in his praise of Tom Brady and the Patriots, while getting ready to join Joe Buck for Fox Network telecast of the Patriots-Giants Super Bowl XLII. But he also issued a caveat regarding the Giants that was prophetic in the sense that it painted the Giants as worthy opponents of the Patriots and certainly capable of winning the game despite the odds against them. "In a strange way," said Aikman, "the Giants have the Patriots to thank for the reason they're in the Super Bowl. I do believe the Giants got better after that season finale. If they had not been playing the Patriots in the final game of the season, in all likelihood a number of their starters wouldn't have been playing in that game. The Giants had not been playing great football, at least offensively, going into that last game. The fact that they were playing New England and New England was going for an undefeated season made the Giants a better team and ultimately landed them in the Super Bowl."

Aikman, certainly a superstar of his era, heaped this praise on Brady and what makes him a great player: "I don't know that I've been around a superstar quarterback who's so in touch with everyone in that locker-room. That's one of the real keys to his success. I've never met his mother and father, but you can tell they're good people and they've done a great job raising him. He's very conscientious and considerate with his time. He handles the media the same way he treats his teammates. They all want a piece of him. And that's hard to do."

Aikman added: "What's impressive about this team to me is it's gotten better while getting younger in a lot of areas (overall a younger average age team than his Cowboys, Steelers, and 49ers were in their championship years). Take the offensive line. Matt Light is the oldest among starters at age 29. If they win the Super Bowl, you can make a valid argument that this is the greatest team of all-time. But I don't see this as being it for them. I see them continuing to be very good for a long time."

Aikman was asked if he viewed this Patriots-Giants collision in the same way as other Boston-New York rivalries. "I don't get the sense that this plays into the same feeling as Yankees-Red Sox," he replied. "It's a lot different feeling, though Bill Belichick cut his teeth with the Giants."

Gil Santos and Gino Cappelletti expected the Patriots to return to their dominant ways of early-season and post a comfortable Super Bowl victory over the Giants. "I think the game will be fairly close in the first half, but then the Patriots will win going away," forecast Santos. He noted Arizona's warm weather would bring "ideal conditions that will provide a distinct advantage for the Patriots with that wide-open offense."

Cappelletti agreed, saying: "I think the team is ready to break it open again and I don't know if the Giants can match their tempo. I believe the Patriots' focus, preparation, and intensity will prevail. The Patriots will score in the 30s and the Giants somewhere in the 20s."

Though the media overplayed Brady's slight ankle injury from the AFC title triumph over San Diego, Santos thought coach Bill Belichick handled the situation well. "The team low-keyed it throughout the week. You know he'll be sharp anyway, but the team was wisely cautious about what was said. But a circus is what happens when the media latches onto a situation like that."

Santos felt another game-deciding factor would be Super Bowl experience. "The Patriots have 21 players who've played in this game before, the Giants just three," he said. Further, the Patriots were looking for their fourth Super Bowl success in seven years.

Before 12 noon Mountain Time on Super Bowl Sunday, the Patriots players and coaches were on their way from their hotel in Scottsdale to the University of Phoenix Stadium in Glendale, a 40-minute bus ride on the interstate 101 loop around Phoenix proper. The 73,000-seat, retractable roof, stadium sits incongruously in Arizona's vast and arid Valley of the Sun, like a giant silver mushroom, or as some people described it, an extraterrestrial "Mother Ship" dwarfing everything around it. The state-of-the-art facility has the first retractable playing surface ever designed for a football stadium, mounted on a vast platform that allows the natural turf to receive the abundant Arizona sunlight (and occasional Arizona rain) when rolled out of the semi-enclosed stadium.

The WBCN broadcast team joined the rest of the Patriots' entourage on the last buses to leave the hotel at 1:00. As usual, the technical crew made sure they entered the stadium at least several hours before that to set up the transmission equipment and to make any necessary adjustments.

The broadcast booths were located high above the field, and between the 30-yard line and the end zone on the AFC side of the stadium. The rest of the media facilities were located high above the end zone. The sight lines were difficult mainly because of the great distance above the playing surface and were problematic when the action was taking place in the far end zone. The AFC booth occupied by WBCN was situated well away from midfield—above and in line with the five-yard line. The NFC (Giants) radio network booth was located to the right of WBCN, even further away from the action. To the left of Gil and Gino was the network television broadcast booth stretching comfortably closer to the 50-yard line. The radio broadcasters had to work the game from such a bad location that Santos quipped that if they were any farther away, "the game would be a rumor."

As Gil and Gino went over their notes before the game, they were invited to join Gary Tanguay and Andy Gresh who were doing their pregame show from the rear section of the booth. With the Patriots favored by two touchdowns to defeat the New York Giants for a second time in little over a month, Gino had no idea how prophetic he was when he commented on the show "that *sometimes a football takes unexpected bounces*." After he and Gil Santos predicted a clear-cut Patriot triumph and the NFL's first perfect 19–0 season and postseason, Cappelletti injected this warning: "The concerns are a good or bad bounce can reflect on the outcome. That's why they play the game."

Little did he know—as Santos indicated he'd love the game to end with "my favorite play, the kneel-down"—that the game-turning *bounce* would be a bizarre late third-down play in which Giants quarterback Eli Manning somehow escaped three Patriots rushers and flung a desperation pass for a 32-yard circus catch by David Tyree. After Manning followed four plays later by lofting a 13-yard winning touchdown pass to Plaxico Burress, who'd ironically predicted the Giants' upset of the NFL's best team, it was clear how important this bizarre play was. Jarvis Green and Richard Seymour had Manning trapped, Green had him by the arm with Adalius Thomas close by, but Manning proved an incredible escape artist. And Tyree leapt, and balanced the pass on his helmet as he fell at the Pats' 24 with safety Rodney Harrison, who tried to pry the ball free. Tyree had completed the astounding connection.

Up in the WBCN booth, located in that terrible high end zone location that was nearly as frustrating as the game, Santos noted Green had Manning "by the back of his shirt." He said Manning "appeared to be sacked." Cappelletti focused on the catch and used the words "unbelievable" and "flabbergasted," the latter describing his own reaction and that of his listening audience as Manning escaped and Tyree held on to the desperation heave of his quarterback.

"You know I shouted out 'He caught it!' but I wasn't totally sure because it was at an angle that it happened," said Cappelletti. "I saw the ball, and arms all over the place, but I didn't see the ball come loose like I expected. As Tyree caught it, he brought it down perfectly pressured against his helmet. I mean he could not have been off a little bit or the ball would have come loose. Wherever he had his pressure against the helmet, it was keeping the ball there. Everybody said that it was a fluke play but there are *always* fluke plays in football. It happened and it was just one great, outstanding play that took place and one that most of the time would not have been a completion."

"The Giants can win the game now," declared Santos after that crucial play. Santos had warned his audience throughout much of the latter part of the game that the Patriots' pursuit of perfection was in serious jeopardy. And sure enough, with 35 seconds left, Giants receiver Plaxico Burress lost Patriots cornerback Ellis Hobbs and snared the decisive 13-yard pass.

Cappelletti later noted, "Boy, they took advantage of that play to Tyree and then popped that touchdown in with ease, with ease! I saw Hobbs stumble, he did stumble, it happened so fast and from the angle I had, I couldn't see if he slipped on the end zone or the one-yard line. So I said that the paint in the end zone sometimes could be slippery. But it was the slip on the cut of Plaxico Burress way before that was the crucial part of the play."

There would be no 19–0 record. Talk of a dynasty was dashed. The Giants would have a 17–14 victory and the NFL championship, and the 1972 Miami Dolphins, who went 17–0, would have the league's only perfect mark.

Now, only the frustrations of the contest would be remembered. On the play before Manning's great escape, corner Asante Samuel seemed to have an interception that would have left the Patriots winners, but the ball deflected off Samuel's reaching fingertips. The Tom Brady-to-Randy Moss come-from-behind touchdown pass of six yards with 2:42 to go in the game looked like it would be the winning score and had excited Santos, who shouted "Touchdown- Randy Moss!!!" as he called the play. It would have been the perfect finish to a season the aerial duo had largely dominated, but it was not to be.

Then there was the difference of three points—the margin by which the Patriots had *won* each of their previous three Super Bowls over six years. This time they had *lost* by three and some would point to a third-quarter decision by coach Bill Belichick, strangely attired in a brilliant garish red hooded Patriots sweatshirt instead of his usual gray, to disdain a 49-yard field goal attempt. Stephen Gostkowski had been hitting from over 50 yards before the game.

Instead, Belichick opted for a fourth-down-and-13 gamble and Tom Brady, overshooting targets much of the night, fired way over Jabar Gaffney in the end zone. "Not even a chance," reacted Cappelletti. Belichick later said he went for field position instead of the long-distance field goal attempt. Tom Brady, harassed by Michael Strahan, Justin Tuck, and a ferocious Giants pass rush that sacked him five times, had just been dropped for a six-yard loss—another key to the decision.

This was far from the dominant, freewheeling Brady that fans had seen all season. Giants quarterback and the game's eventual MVP, Eli Manning, outplayed the Tom Brady who quarterbacked the Patriots on this day—a Tom Brady that Gino sensed was just not himself. "Something is going on . . . Tom is taking a little longer to throw than I have ever seen him before," Gino noted, and repeated the thought several times during the broadcast.

The relentless pressure of the New York rush got to Brady. His passes sailed high and, except for that late drive toward the touchdown pass to Moss, he couldn't launch a threat after the 56-yard drive at the end of the first period capped by Laurence Maroney's one-yard touchdown on the first play of the second quarter which gave the Patriots a 7–3 lead. That score held up until the fourth quarter, when Manning's five-yard toss netted David Tyree's first touchdown all season and a 10–7 Giant edge with 11:13 to play.

Why was Brady so battered, clearly a key to a Super Bowl upset perhaps bigger than Joe Namath shocking the Baltimore Colts and definitely larger than the Pats jolting St. Louis for their first Super-success in 2001? Cappelletti had thought the huge Justin Tuck and other Giant pass rushers would eventually run out of gas. He wondered even during the first half if they could keep it up. They did.

The Giants stopped the number one offense in NFL history, holding it to its lowest point total of the year. The Patriot offensive line was badly outplayed as the Giants' front wall controlled play—as evidenced by two false starts by Matt Light and one by Benjamin Watson, all in the third period. Light and Nick Kaczur could not protect Brady and neither could usually strong Dan Koppen, Logan Mankins, Stephen Neal (who left with a knee injury in the second quarter), and understudy Russ Hochstein.

The result was poor throws, though Brady completed 29 of 48 for 266 yards and the Moss touchdown. Moss ended with 24 catches, but no Super Bowl ring. The Patriots' big star was Wes Welker, who had 11 receptions for a second straight game. Welker was a big thorn to the Giants, but after Maroney faded and Kevin Faulk went out injured for a while, he was virtually alone. And for a second straight year, a Manning ended the Patriots' hopes—Peyton (Eli's older brother) doing so a year earlier as Indianapolis rallied to win the AFC title game.

Then there were missed opportunities. Ellis Hobbs, beaten for the winning score, earlier intercepted Manning in the Pats' end. But the Patriots couldn't capitalize as Maroney was stopped on second-and-one and third-and-one, and a punt followed. They later didn't take advantage of Belichick winning a challenge that the Giants had 12 men on the field. That gave them a first down at the Giant 39, but Strahan sacked Brady, and Belichick decided not to try for a long field goal and instead opted for a Brady bomb that wound up way off-target.

"I know it's a devastating loss after what the Patriots accomplished, but the Giants played better football, and more consistently," explained Gino immediately following the game. "The Patriots did not play well and the Giants did. The Patriots are a better team, but not today." Not against the "road warrior" Giants, who went on a title tear away from Giants Stadium.

He and Gino agreed that Brady, perhaps bothered by a tender ankle, played below his high standard, missing open targets. And they seemed to agree with Fox analyst Howie Long, the Charlestown native, who said the Patriots had "a false sense of security."

Unlike the euphoria of the Patriots' first Super Bowl victory over the Rams in 2002, it was not a good day to be a New England fan.

"A lot of people predicted that the Giants' defense (number one in the NFL) would make a difference and I have to admit it did," said Santos—a solid punctuation to a sharply disappointing Super Bowl that gave New England fans a deep nauseating feeling for days.

Sixteen regular season wins and no losses is a record that has never been achieved by any team before the Patriots did it in 2007. Eighteen victories and one loss is an incredibly great record. But because that one loss was the *last* loss—a *Super Bowl loss*—it seemed to negate all of the other Patriots victories in the eyes of the football world.

Gil Santos admits to being a Patriots fan first and foremost and being emotionally attached to the play on the field—even as he strives to call the game with honesty and objectivity. But off the air just minutes after the end of the game, Gil asked the rhetorical question that everyone else in the broadcast booth was thinking: "Eighteen and one! Eighteen and one! Why couldn't that one loss have happened last October instead of today?"

Statistician Roger Homan, who sat between Gil and Gino all season long, was the man who kept the numbers and witnessed the incredible achievements of the Patriots this year and in many years past. He brings a perspective and a sense of closure to the 2007–2008 Patriot season that many fans will understand. "First, I took the Super Bowl loss in stride and was not terribly upset. Disappointed? Yes! But I tried to pinch myself all through the season realizing how lucky I was, how lucky we all were at what we were experiencing. We talked about it numerous times. What if we beat Dallas? Can we beat the Colts in Indy? Then after the near defeats against the Eagles and Ravens, all the chips seemed to be falling into place and then the stage was set for three out of four games at home in December that was capped with a thrilling come-from-behind victory over the Giants in the last game.

"We covered a team that went 18–1. If that one loss was any other time *but* the last game of the year, this team would hands down have been at the head of the list of the conversations about who was greatest team ever. Now it can still be in that conversation, but along with conversation about the greatest [regular] season ever will go talk about the greatest loss in the history of the game. The pundits will have their fun proving both sides. I know what I saw and experienced in 2007–2008 was the thrill of a lifetime.

"As you get older in life and realize how fragile our existence is, you wonder if maybe there are a lot of stronger forces in control of the final outcomes."

The convergence of so many unusual factors and happenstances that resulted in the Patriots playing their worst game of the season led Homan to ponder the strange and negative karma apparent to the Patriots and their fans in hindsight. "Brady's injured ankle, the horrible play of the offensive line, coaching decisions uncharacteristic of previous games, interceptions that should have happened but did not, fumble recoveries blown, and the opposing quarterback slipping out of apparent sacks plagued the Pats to the end. Most of all, it was the Giants rising up and playing way over their heads to making Houdini-type conversions and miracle catches by no-name players to complete their own unbelievable season.

"Maybe God is the ultimate sports fan and controls who is going to hit .400, have 56-game hitting streaks, score 100 points in a basketball game, or even have an NFL team be 19–0. Some records are meant never to be broken. In a season where the Patriots shattered NFL and team records this is one where they grasped at football immortality but could not hold on.

"I counted my blessings through the entire year at how special this season was and what I was able to witness up close. What I take away from this year are memories that will live as long as there is football. The 2007 Patriots, to those of us that saw them week in and week out, know they were the greatest. This team allowed me to experience and witness history and appreciate their individual and team accomplishments at the highest levels ever achieved," concluded the Pats' "ace" statistician.

And what were Gino's comments about this one game and its impact on the Patriots? He shared the following thoughts a few weeks after the end of the season. "When you talk about 'big' games... I don't know that there has ever been a game as 'big' as what the 2008 Super Bowl meant. I think that's part of the hurt. That game was built up to mean so much in and of itself. That one game was all there was left following the greatest season that the Patriots had ever had, and everything seemed to hinge on winning it or the season was not considered complete or successful in the eyes of many people. What it grew to mean in the history of the franchise and in football history was almost unreasonable. To achieve an undefeated season is something that is truly remarkable.

"The style of play that they displayed all season long certainly would have qualified them as one of the truly elite teams in the history of professional football had that one loss not occurred. I think all that was on the table before the game and to have that much at stake, having one game mean so much, is almost unrealistic. They shouldn't have a game that big—it meant too much. It meant the Super Bowl, it meant finishing off a glorious season, and it meant going down in history as one of the most elite teams in professional football. If you thought about the meaning of this game, I can see where you might just lose a little focus as a player. All the games that they have played and won and yet they had to win one more or the season and their record didn't mean anything? I don't think that seems fair."

Gino went on to describe the cruel paradox of such a great season and the disappointing Super Bowl defeat. "What happened was that the loss in the Super Bowl tarnished the season, and prevented them from going down in history as an undefeated and untied team. The disappointment was disastrous, yet you *cannot* say the season was a disaster, because of that incredible record and all the things that were done so well during the season. Truly it was a *disappointing* loss. I could just feel for what those players were thinking and what they had to do."

Since the Patriots' season of 2003, the team has won 66 regular season games and have lost just 14. During that same stretch, they have been in the playoffs five times including three Super Bowls—and have won two out of three of them. The overall Patriot record from September 7, 2003 to February 3, 2008 has been an astonishing 77 victories against only 17 losses. Every year the Patriots' coaching staff and ownership have put together a team that has generally proven stronger and better than the previous team. It seems clear that there will continue to be much to cheer about. There will be other games, other seasons, other victories, other championships and Patriots fans look forward to Gil Santos and Gino Cappelletti telling them all about it.

14
SIGN OFF

"In my mind, Gil is the Patriots. He's Johnny Most with a different style. I live in the New York area and I follow the Patriots on satellite radio. I've been following Gil and Gino's broadcasts for a long time and I think they're wonderful. They work so well together, you feel while listening to them that they really like each other!"—**MIKE GORMAN**, CELTICS COMCAST TELEVISION ANNOUNCER TEAMED WITH TOM HEINSOHN FOR 27 YEARS

"Santos and Cappelletti are fascinating to me. I love Gil's voice, which has become the spirit of football in New England. I grew up listening to this guy and that voice was on a record that I had of the 1976 team. Gino, who belongs in the Hall of Fame, just plays off Gil so well. They know the game and they've called so many meaningful games through the years. They've called the Patriots' fortunes through the down and up years and the nice thing is they have never changed. They're great guys. And they don't shine the spotlight on themselves. They are something special!"—**STEVE BURTON**, WBZ-TV CHANNEL 4 SPORTS REPORTER

GIL: "As I said before, working beside and with Gino is like slipping on an old shoe. I am comfortable on the air with Gino. We play off each other very well. Neither one of us is so ego driven that we want to be the show, because the game is the show. Gino has a great sense of timing as to when to come in and explain why a play did or did not work...whether it's offense...defense or special teams...he just has a really good feel for it. The other thing I find very valuable is that because of his vast experience as a player and a coach, he can tell very early in a game if the Patriots or their opponents are not 'up' for the game. He has an innate ability to spot that quickly, something that most fans, myself included, don't really pick up on—and I think that is an invaluable asset.

"The truth of the matter is, I would work with Gino and call the Patriots games for free. Sometimes I just sit and say to myself that I am astounded that I can sit at the 50-yard line of every Patriots game and broadcast and talk about the game with my friend—and I am getting paid to do it! It's the most wonderful job in the world whether we are winning or losing.

"Let me tell you winning is a heck of a lot more fun! It's a lot easier broadcasting when the team is winning, because the team is carrying the broadcast which is the way it should be.

"It's just fun. It's three hours of on the air fun, if it ends up in victory all the better. If it ends up in defeat, you know it takes away some of the fun. But it is the greatest job in the world nonetheless. And I am just so comfortable with Gino, he's like my brother only we don't fight. Brothers argue, we have never had an argument. It is just a wonderful, wonderful way to make a living and I feel very, very fortunate."

GINO: "It certainly has been a great ride for me to be able to have these different perspectives of the franchise and I have enjoyed the time I have been somewhat identified with the team as a player, as a broadcaster, then a little stint as a coach, and then back to broadcasting.

"When Gil first interviewed me for the job, I just found a simpatico that still exists today. It was instant as to how we did the game at the studio audition. We were in a little dark room at WBZ where they threw a film of a game up on a screen and Gil did the play by play and I did the comments. Of course they were interviewing different guys—former players—to be possible color analysts for Gil's play-by-play broadcasts. Gil chose me which I was very appreciative of at the time and continue to appreciate that now because I have been clinging to his coattails ever since!

"We just have had so many experiences that we share. Sometimes we don't even have to say anything to each other, and we know exactly what the other is thinking.

"In my mind, and I have listened to plenty of broadcasts, there is no question that Gil is the consummate play-by-play radio football announcer in the entire country. And I say that because of listening to him as a fan as well as working with him as professional. His accuracy, his way, and his style are things that belong only to Mister Gil Santos. He has always been totally prepared—always. These are the things you admire. He has been a hard working guy all his life, in every one of his endeavors, and it comes through in the broadcast.

"I'd have to say that, of the overall time I have had with the Patriots, the broadcasting part is playing as big a part as my playing days with me being identified with the team. I can honestly say that the broadcasting has maintained my identity with the franchise and as a player as well. A lot of players would lose that once they left football and left the team and went back someplace to a job or other career outside of the game. I was very fortunate to retain that association with pro football and the Patriots this way."

APPENDIX I
THE MAN IN THE MIDDLE—ROGER HOMAN, WBCN / PATRIOTS ROCK RADIO NETWORK STATISTICIAN

ROGER HOMAN has been the official game day broadcast statistician of the New England Patriots for 19 years, providing game details to dozens of national network broadcasting crews He has been sitting between Gil and Gino since 1971 during their first tenure and joined them again in 2000 for the WBCN/Patriots Rock Radio Network.

"Well, when you work with so many different people, you see what detail Gil and Gino put into a broadcast. Gil prepares like no one else. He has every single possible statistic about a player, records they have set, possible records they might set, and where they rank. He has field goal percentages from every ten-yard stripe, I mean nobody that I have worked with prepares like that. They expect somebody else to do that, whether it's the spotter they hire, or the statistician they would hire, whatever.

"He's on top of things to the point where we've worked so long and so well together that I don't even waste time double-checking a certain statistic he may bring into the broadcast.

As the game goes on, someone from the Patriots staff comes in the booth with their quarter-by-quarter printouts of what possible records may be going to be set. So, if somebody has passed somebody in the Patriots record book, or in the NFL record book, I make sure Gil gets that information in a timely manner. But we usually have gotten to it first.

"There could be an obscure record that was broken, for instance in a game where Ben Watson received two touchdown passes, that tied Stanley Morgan. I wouldn't have known that, but somebody punched it up and the guy who does the running gave us that number. Those things come in—sometimes it's added fodder, sometimes it's not.

"Then you get a sense for each game, for instance Brady had 13 complete passes in a row in a game. When you start getting into those things, you start thinking that could be a record. Or when you get near 30 first downs for a team, that's probably near a record. Or, somebody gets 150 yards receiving, you just have a sixth sense that this might be leading to a record. That is when the Patriots media guide comes into play—so you can quickly look up those kinds of records. The guide has a convenient section called "the Last Time." You know the last time somebody ran for 200 yards, or the last time that someone did something. You can look those things up very quickly during the broadcast.

"The last five or six games of the season, my job becomes much more intense because almost every play is potentially a record being broken. Obviously once they have broken that record, every time they do it again, it's rewriting the books. But it's fun, it's an absolute blast—it keeps me really, really focused, in tune as we try to keep up with everything. We want to break it at the same time at least, if not ahead of anybody else.

"If I hear Gil talking about a specific stat, I will write it down so I can feed him [it]. At the approach of halftime during the Jacksonville play-off game, we realized that there were only two incompletions in the game at that point. Brady was perfect and Jacksonville had two incomplete passes. So Gino used that information and gave me credit for it at halftime.

"Gino is generally much more independent regarding relying on me for stats. He's an icon, he's a Hall of Famer—if not at the moment, he should be soon—he's the one we respect so much. It's a travesty that he is not in the pro football Hall of Fame. There are some things going on to rectify that—when you look at the records and the time, the era that he played, there is no question that he belongs in the Hall of Fame.

"Gino gives the broadcast a player's perspective versus Gil who is much more of a numbers guy who paints the picture. And Gil has a way of taking the numbers and making them sound important—it's not just arbitrary numbers, you know Brady is this, and this, and this. It's *What about this, fans?* Tom Brady is *13 for 13* in the *first half* with a *hundred and eighty* yards! He knows how to put the emphasis behind his words and the numbers—he knows how to make the numbers important. He always uses them to flower and make a point that he has started. I can fill him in with the numbers that he's looking to use to make his point.

"Gillette Stadium in Foxboro is an ideal setup—some of the stadiums we have to work in are incredible. We are sometimes really cramped—sometimes you have obstacles in front of you. You sometimes have fans so close in front of you that when they stand up, you can't see the field. You do some games in some places from the end zone. There are some real challenges to get the broadcast out—there is nobody that does it better than Gil.

"That's what a good play-by-play man does—you can close your eyes and you can visualize the action. If you know the sport, it's even easier. Gil has always pointed out that you have to assume the person that you are broadcasting to doesn't always know everything. So some of the obvious and mundane types of things still have to be brought in to keep that listener involved. And then you have to go into a little more depth to keep those who are more sophisticated about the sport saying, 'boy, that's great!'

"It's always difficult from a play-by-play point of view to always see who made the first hit, or who made the tackle, or who deflected a pass, or interception or whatever. Gino's right on top of that.

"Part of my job is to fill in the call for Gil when he is trying to figure out the exact call on some confusing plays. Gil is always concentrating on watching the ball when the players go into a pile, or when the ball goes into a congested area of the field, and I'm trying to fill in some of the details for him. Many times Gino has already picked up on it before I can even get to Gil. They are such natural complements to each other. There are really not a lot of staged kinds of things during the broadcast. It just flows naturally.

"Gino, Gil, Marc Cappello, and I eat together all the time. When you are sitting with two Hall of Fame quality professionals, the opinions and comments of Marc and me are always considered and respected. Who would have a better opinion than Gil? Who would have a better perspective from a player's point of view than Gino?

"We all work together—Marc Cappello is kind of a dinosaur in that he is so young but fits in so well because he has the ability to relate to the Cappelletti generation and the prominence of a Gil Santos in the booth. And Dennis Knudsen is the same way. When I came back in 2000, the two things I was most impressed with was how young Marc and Dennis were but yet how professional they were. They understood who is working with them. They are so professional in what they do—it's very, very impressive.

"Dennis is a phenomenal engineer—we used to play games and tried to screw up his board. You have seen the knobs on that audio board—there are a million knobs, and I'd screw with something and he'd turn around and find what I did to that board in a second. He's just absolutely amazing. It is a pleasure to work with him and the entire 'BCN crew."

GIL AND GINO'S GOURMET GUIDE
to their favorite restaurants in and around the cities of the NFL°

Atlanta
Bone's Restaurant a/k/a **Bone's Steak House**, 3130 Piedmont Rd., NE
(404) 237-2663. www.bonesrestaurant.com
"It's one of the best steak houses in America, very popular with the sports
crowd."—Gino. Gil says, "Amen."

Baltimore
Tio Pepe's, 10 E Franklin St. (410) 539-4675.
coloquio.com/coloquioonline/tiopepe.htm
"Spanish restaurant in a white-washed cellar setting. Excellent paella."—Gil

Pierpoints, 1822 Aliceanna St. (410) 675-2080.
"Seafood at its best. Think crab when you are in Baltimore."—Gino

Boston / Providence
For great Italian food, "The North End in Boston or Atwells Avenue in
Providence. Take your pick, you can't go wrong."—Gino

Buffalo
EB Green's Steakhouse, Hyatt Regency Buffalo, 2 Fountain Plz.
(716) 855-4870. www.ebgreens.com

Charlotte
Sullivan's Steakhouse, 1928 South Boulevard, Suite 200 (704) 335-8228.
www.sullivansteakhouse.com/charlotte
"Great steaks...great service...great cocktails."—Gil

Chicago
Gene and Georgetti's Steakhouse, 500 N Franklin St. (312) 527-3718.
www.geneandgeorgetti.com
"From the outside it looks like an Italian-American or Portugese-Ameri-
can men's club...the steaks are fabulous and a side order of pasta with
meat sauce is a must."—Gil

Harry Caray's, 33 W. Kinzie St. (773) HOLY-COW. www.harrycarays.com

---

°Gil, Gino, and the authors of this book cannot assure the quality or anyone else's satisfaction with
the establishments listed. We present this guide simply as a listing of the personal dining preferences
of Gil and Gino. The addresses and contact information is believed to be correct and up to date as
of the publication date of this book. You should contact each establishment to ensure that the information regarding operation, location, and specialties mentioned are accurate.

Cincinnati

Mortons–The Steakhouse, 441 Vine St. # 2A. (513) 241-4104.
www.mortons.com
"Can't go wrong...a big local favorite that we've found."—Gil

Montgomery Inn Boathouse, 925 Riverside Dr. (513) 721-7427.
www.montgomeryinn.com. "BBQ at its best."—Gino

Cleveland

Baricelli Inn, 2203 Cornell Rd. (216) 791-6500. www.baricelli.com
"Located in an elegant 1896 mansion in Little Italy—outstanding. Tell
owner Paul Minnillo greetings from New England."—Gino

Dallas

The Palm, 701 Ross Ave. (214) 698-0470. www.thepalm.com
"If in Texas...eat steak....I really like The Palm. "—Gil

Pappas Brothers Steakhouse, 10477 Lombardy Ln.
(214) 366-2000. www.pappasbros.com

Detroit

Carl's Chop House, 3020 Grand River Ave. (313) 833-0700.
www.carlschophouse.com

Houston

Vic and Anthony's Steakhouse, 1510 Texas St.
(713) 228-1111. www.vicandanthonys.com
"The best steak au poivre anywhere! Great lounge and dining ambi-
ence."—Gino

Indianapolis

St. Elmo Steakhouse, 127 S Illinois St. (317) 635-0636. www.stelmos.com
"Terrific steaks and the best Navy Bean soup going...if you like spicy, get
their fire-alarm shrimp cocktail sauce."—Gil

Canterbury Hotel, 123 S Illinois St. (317) 634-3000.
www.canterburyhotel.com
"For fine dining, try the Canterbury Hotel across the street from St.
Elmo."—Gino

Jacksonville

Mezza Luna, 110 1st St., Neptune Beach, FL
(904) 249-5573. www.mezzalunaneptunebeach.com

Kansas City

Hereford House, 2 East 20th St. (816) 842-1080. www.herefordhouse.com
"If you are thinking great steak in KC."—Gino

Miami

Joe's Stone Crab, 11 Washington Ave. (305) 673-0365.
www.joesstonecrab.com
Note: "Reservations are a must."—Gino

Jackson's Steakhouse, 450 East Las Olas Blvd., Fort Lauderdale, FL
954-522-4450. www.jacksonssteakhouse.com
"Owned and operated by a Wareham native...ask for Jack...tell him
you're from New England and he'll treat you like a king...great steaks...
top shelf all around."—Gill

Green Bay

The 5th Quarter, 2101 American Dr., Little Chute, WI
(920) 687-9751. www.5thquarter@5thquartersportsbar.com
"You pick out your own steak from the meat case and char grill it yourself
on a giant charcoal pit in the middle of the room."—Gil

Minneapolis

"I'll let Gino do this one since he's a Golden Gopher."—Gil

Jax Café, 1928 University Ave NE (612) 789-7297. www.jaxcafe.com

Manny's Steakhouse, Hyatt Regency, 1300 Nicollet Mall
(612) 339-9900. www.mannyssteakehouse.com

Tejas, 3910 W. 50th St., Edina, MN (952) 926-0800.
www.tejasrestaurant.com
"If in the suburbs, try Tejas."—Gino

Nashville

Restaurant Zola, 3001 W End Ave. (615) 320-7778. restaurantzola.com

Sunset Grill, 2001 Belcourt Ave. (615) 386-3663. www.sunsetgrill.com

New Orleans

Emeril's New Orleans, 800 Tchoupitoulas St. (504) 528-9393.

Emeril's Delmonico, 1300 Saint Charles Ave. (504) 525-4937.

Emeril's Nola, 829 Saint Charles Ave. (504) 558-3940. www.emerils.com
"Throw a rock...whatever restaurant you hit will be good...I am partial
to home boy Emeril's places...he has three of them. All great."—Gil

Bayona, 430 Dauphine St. (504) 525-4455. www.bayona.com
"In the heart of New Orleans, tell Susan Gino sent you."—Gino

New York

Tribeca Grill, 375 Greenwich St. (212) 941-3900.
www.myriadrestaurantgroup.com
"In the city it's the Tribeca Grill for me."—Gino

Bice Ristorante, 7 E 54th St. (close to the Waldorlf Astoria) (212) 752-1329. www.bicenewyork.com

Il Villaggio Restaurant, 651 State Rt. 17, Carlstadt, NJ (201) 935-7733. www.ilvillaggio.com
"We stay in New Jersey and since discovering Il Villagio on Rt 17 just a few miles from our hotel we look forward to going every year... The pasta fagoli is the best I've ever tasted."—Gil

Oakland

Olieito Restaurant, 5655 College Ave. (510) 547-5356. www.oliveto.com

Citron, 5484 College Ave. (510) 653-5484. www.citronrestaurant.com

Philadelphia

Bookbinders, 125 Walnut St. (215) 925-7027. www.bookbinders.biz

Jack's Firehouse, 2130 Fairmount Ave. (215) 232-9000. www.jacksfirehouse.com

Phoenix

Tarbells, 3213 E. Camelback Rd. (602) 955-8100. www.tarbells.com

Biltmore Grill, 2400 E Missouri Ave. (602) 954-2518. www.arizonabiltmore.com

Pittsburgh

Mallorca Restaurant, 2228 E. Carson Street, South side (412) 488-1818. www.mallorcarestaurant.com/
"Imagine my surprise when I found this place... Portuguese and Spanish cooking... in PITTSBURGH! It's outstanding... ask for Antonio."—Gil

Tambellini's Ristorante, 139 7th St. (414) 391-1091. www.eatzucchini.com
"Been going there for years... always great."—Gino

Abrio Restaurant, 94 Center Church Rd. Canonsburg, PA (724) 941-8424. www.abriorestaurant.com

St. Louis

Cardwell's at the Plaza, at 97 Plaza Sq. (314) 997-8885. www.cardwellsattheplaza.com

Charlie Gitto's Italian Restaurant (On The Hill), 206 North 6th St. (314) 772-8898. www.charliegittos.com
"Recommended to us by Tom Lasorda—great tip."—Gino

San Diego

Island Prime, 880 Harbor Island Dr. (619) 298-6802. www.cohnrestaurants.com

Blue Point Coastal Cusine, 565 5th Ave. (downtown in Gas Light section) (619) 233-6623. www.cohnrestaurants.com

San Francisco

Boulevard Restaurant, 1 Mission St.
(415) 543-6084. www.boulevardrestaurant.com
"Excellent!"—Gil
"Best fried calamari ever!"—Gino

Rubicon Restaurant, 558 Sacramento St.
(413) 434-4100. www.sfrubicon.com
"Robin Williams, Francis Ford Coppola and Robert DeNiro's restaurant. A very interesting place with a very eclectic menu."—Gino

Seattle

Metropolitan Grille, 820 2nd Ave. (206) 624-3287. www.themetropolitangrill.com

Tampa

The Columbia House, 2117 E 7th Ave.
(813) 248-4961. www.columbiarestaurant.com
"It's touristy but I like it…old world Spanish."—Gil

Berns World Famous Steakhouse, 1208 S. Howard Ave.
(813) 251-2421. www.bernssteakhouse.com
"It has the biggest wine list you have ever seen! And you pay for your steak by the thickness in inches of each cut!"Gil

Donatello, 232 N. Dale Mabry Hwy. (813) 875-6660.
www.donatellorestaurant.com
"Northern Italian specialties."—Gino

Washington, DC

Kinkade's Steak and Seafood, 2000 Pennsylvania Ave NW.
(202) 296-7700. www.kinkead.com
"Very good seafood place…Gino found it."—Gil

APPENDIX III
HALL-OF-FAME WORTHY CAREERS

GINO CAPPELLETTI AND GIL SANTOS have contributed to professional football and to sports broadcasting at the highest levels. Some of their notable achievements are summarized here.

Gil Santos' Career Highlights

- 59 years as a radio broadcaster

- 42 years on Boston radio

- 37 years as a radio sports reporter and anchor on WBZ AM for "The WBZ Morning News"

- Prior to working at WBZ Radio Santos worked at WBSM and WNBH Radio in New Bedford, Massachusetts, and WSAR and WALE Radio in Fall River, Massachusetts from 1959 to 1971

- 32 years as the voice of the New England Patriots

- 25 years teamed with Gino Cappelletti as the Patriots radio broadcasting team

- 10 years as the radio and television broadcaster of the Boston Celtics from 1980 to 1990

- Announced Boston College Football for 13 years on radio and for three years on television

- Play-by-play for:
  New England Teamen soccer
  Providence College basketball
  Brown University football
  Penn State football
  CBS-TV NFL football
  ABC-TV and radio football
  The 1984 ABC and WLVI-TV Olympic broadcast
  The Boston Marathon (37 years)
  Big East TV basketball

- Four-time winner of Massachusetts Sportscaster of the year

- A New England Emmy Award winner in 1978 for Boston College vs. Stanford Play-by-Play

- Four Massachusetts Sportscaster of the Year Awards

- 25 Associated Press Best Play-by-Play Awards, Marathon, and Sports Reporting

- A UPI Best New England Sportscaster Award

- Four National United Press International Tom Phillips Awards for best sports casting including one for the Boston Marathon, and another for the best football play-by-play in America

- Inducted into The Sports Museum Hall of Fame in 2004 with a Legacy Award

- Inducted in 2002 to the Fairhaven High School Hall of Fame

Gino Cappelletti's Career Highlights*

- Selected as a halfback and kicker on the Minnesota High School All-State football team

- University of Minnesota quarterback and place-kicker

- Original member of the Boston Patriots in the American Football League 1960 played two positions each season defensive back/kicker 1960, offensive receiver/kicker 1962–1970

- Scored the first field goal and points in AFL and Patriots history

- AFL Most Valuable Player in 1964 (runner up in 1961 to George Blanda)

- Led the AFL in scoring as a wide receiver and place kicker five times (1961, 1963, 1964, 1965, 1966)

- Led the Patriots in scoring for 10 consecutive seasons (1960–1969)

- Holds the top two scoring season records with the AFL (1961: 147 pts.; 1964: 155 points)

- Scored more than 100 points per season for six straight seasons (1961–1966)

- First AFL player to score more than 1,000 points (record established on a 19-yard TD catch November 10, 1968)

- All-time AFL scoring leader with 1,130 points (42 TDs, 176 FGs, and 342 PATs)

- Only one of three AFL players to play in every game in the AFL's 10-year history (the other two were George Blanda and Jim Otto)

---

* It should be noted that all of Gino's professional football records and accomplishments were achieved during a 14-game season (as opposed to the current 16-game season). In addition, there was no overtime rule for tie games, thus the opportunity for additional point scoring was dramatically reduced, especially in regard to field goals (during Gino's career nine of his games ended in ties). Finally, the opportunity for postseason play and thus additional statistics was limited to a single postseason championship game. Today, the extended playoff system could add as many as many as four postseason games per year to a player's career.

- Five time AFL All-Star (equivalent of today's Pro-Bowl) as wide receiver and kicker

- Patriot leading receiver in 1961 (768 yds. 17.1 avg.), and 1964 (864 yds. 17.7 avg.)

- Is the Patriot record holder for:
  Most points scored in a season (155 in 1964)
  Most points scored in one game (28 vs. Houston, Dec. 16, 1965)
  Most seasons leading the league in scoring (5—1961, 1963, 1964, 1965, 1966)
  Most field goal attempts in a career (334)
  Most field goals made in a game

- Holds all time pro-football record of 7.5 points scored per game average over 11 years

- Established pro football record with six field goals in one game (vs. Denver in 1964), also had no misses in that game.

- Voted by fans to the Patriots 10th Anniversary Team (1971)

- New England Patriots Hall of Fame (1992)

- Selected by media as wide receiver and as kicker to the Patriots 35th Anniversary Team (1994)

- Selected by fans to the Patriots Team of the Century as wide receiver and as kicker (2000)

- National Italian-American Sports Hall of Fame (1984)

- Special teams coach for the Patriots for three years (1979–81)

- Sportscaster WCOP Radio / Sports anchor for WBZ TV

- Radio broadcaster and analyst for the Patriots for 28 years

See the following web sites information regarding criteria for induction, or for general information regarding the American Sportscasters Association Hall of Fame and the Professional Football Hall of Fame

American Sportscasters Association Hall of Fame
   www.americansportscasters.com/halloffame.html

Professional Football Hall of Fame
   www.profootballhof.com

A NOTE ON SOURCES

Most of the material in this book was gathered through personal interviews conducted by the authors with the many individuals whose comments and remarks appear in the text. Additional data, records, and other statistics concerning Gil Santos, Gino Cappelletti, and the New England Patriots are attributable to various editions of the *New England Patriots Media Guide*, and other official publications of the New England Patriots organization. Likewise, records, statistics, and data concerning other NFL teams, coaches, or players are attributable to personal interviews, individual team media publications, and through the NFL's publications, media communications, press conferences, and press releases.

The vast body of knowledge of author Jim Baker acquired as a sports reporter and columnist for the *Buffalo Courier-Express* and the *Boston Herald* for over 40 years is an integral part of this book as is the experience of author Chuck Burgess as a Patriots fan for 48 years!

INDEX

Authors Chuck Burgess and Jim Baker. Photo by Michael Allen